Getting Into Australia

howtobooks

Please send for a free copy of the latest catalogue:

How To Books
3 Newtec Place, Magdalen Road,
Oxford OX4 1RE, United Kingdom
email: info@howtobooks.co.uk
http://www.howtobooks.co.uk

Getting Into
Australia

The complete immigration guide to
gaining a short or long-term visa

2nd edition

MATHEW COLLINS

Published by How To Books Ltd,
3 Newtec Place, Magdalen Road,
Oxford OX4 1RE. United Kingdom.
Tel: (01865) 793806. Fax: (01865) 248780.
email: info@howtobooks.co.uk
http://www.howtobooks.co.uk

First edition 2001
Reprinted 2003
Second edition 2005

British Library Cataloguing in Publication Data
A catalogue record for this book is available from the British
Library

Cover design by Baseline Arts Ltd, Oxford
Produced for How To Books by Deer Park Productions, Tavistock
Typeset by PDQ Typesetting, Newcastle-under-Lyme
Printed and bound by Cromwell Press, Trowbridge, Wiltshire

NOTE: The material contained in this book is set out in good
faith for general guidance and no liability can be accepted
for loss or expense incurred as a result of relying in particular
circumstances on statements made in the book. The laws and
regulations are complex and liable to change, and readers should
check the current position with the relevant authorities before
making personal arrangements.

Contents

AMBLER COLLINS
IMMIGRATION & COMMERCIAL CONSULTANTS

Dear Reader

Thank you for reading my book.

This probably means that you have some interest in migrating to New Zealand and want to know about starting a new life in a new country.

New Zealand has its own immigration legislation, policies and procedures. These policies are usually reviewed, changed and fine tuned by them on an annual basis.

Your application will have individual circumstances which will be unique to you.
Factors taken into consideration can include your qualifications, work experience, training, age, capital resources, family relations and business experience, to name just some.
The process can be long and costly and very disappointing if you get it wrong.

So how do you know if you will qualify?

The first step in any migration strategy is to have your personal circumstances assessed against the various categories and criteria to determine your suitability.

My company, AmblerCollins Visa Specialists was established in the early 1990's and is the longest established multi-destinational visa consultancy in the UK. Over the years we have helped many thousands of clients achieve their dream of starting a new life in a new country. If it is possible to get you to your country of choice we will definitely get you there.

As a way of saying thank you please feel free to take up my **FREE ASSESSMENT OFFER**.

Good Luck

M. 7. Coll.

Mathew Collins

*To take advantage of our Free Assessment offer please e-mail to: **info@amblercollins.com***
In your email please include "How To Books - Free Assessment Offer" in the subject line or
*call me or one of my team on **020 7371 0213***

Eden House, 59 Fulham High Street, London SW6 3JJ Telephone: (020) 7371 0213 Fax: (020) 7736 8841
e-mail: info@amblercollins.com   Internet http://www.abmblercollins.com

Preface

Australia is one of the most multicultural countries in the world and has proven to be extremely popular with both holidaymakers and those looking for a complete lifestyle change. Australia's population has been enhanced by nearly every nationality, making Australia's vast landscapes a melting pot of cultural diversity, changing societies and dynamic economies.

Amongst these constant changes, Australia's immigration policies have been the subject of constant analysis and updating. I have written this book in an attempt to simplify current immigration policies and procedures in a way that will allow you to understand the implications of these policies and what they mean to you.

Having practised immigration consultancy for almost 15 years, I have found that most people ask the same questions: 'How do I migrate to Australia?' 'How long does it take?' and 'How much does it cost?'

Immigration, like most government policies and laws, is a complex subject to tackle. Most clients want to know the steps required to immigrate, what documentation is required, what are the best channels to use and what are their chances of success.

This book discusses staying in Australia temporarily and permanently, family categories, employer sponsored categories, setting up in business, business skills and investment categories. I have included useful contacts that you can use to obtain the latest up-to-date information and documentation for your application.

In today's new electronic world and marketplace, the global traveller and company are driving and increasing the demand for people who will live in a different geographical location. The advent of email and the internet is contributing to the need and demand for accurate immigration information.

Completing this book has been a challenge. Alongside managing a busy practice and the day-to-day demands of our clients this has been a task that would not have been completed without the assistance of Nicky Barclay, my colleague and workmate. Nicky has spent many hours on the research and compilation of material for this hand-book; without her this project would still be on my hard drive. Her dedication and application in assisting in the completion of this project has allowed the book to get to print. For this she has my gratitude, appreciation and respect.

After reading this book, you will be confident enough to be able to handle your own case or be able to tell your visa consultant what you hope to accomplish.

Good luck!

Australia's History

A NATION IS BORN

Until fairly recently, Australian immigration policies encouraged British applications for permanent residency and citizenship. As a consequence almost everyone in the UK seems to have at least one relative living in Australia. In the early days of colonial rule, the British government used Australia as an outlet to hold their convicts. On the 26th of January 1788 the first fleet of 11 ships arrived at Sydney Harbour and this marked the beginning of a new nation. A second coastal penal settlement was established in Tasmania in 1825. From the first colony, exploration and settlement spread and at the same time the British government was giving away free land in order to encourage people to move away from the overcrowded shores of Britain to the apparently empty land of Australia.

Free settlers started to greatly outnumber the convict population and settlements spread to South Australia in 1837. Victoria sprang up in 1851, Queensland in 1859 and although the Swan River Colony had been established in 1827 it only became a self-governing colony in 1890. The Commonwealth of Australia was formed in 1901 through the proclamation of the Constitution for the Federation of six States. The original fathers knew that they were at the forefront of this new nation and were concerned about avoiding the pitfalls of the lands that they had come from. They had progressive ideas about the rights of man, democratic procedures and the value of a secret ballot. Since then the constitutional links with Britain have been slowly loosened.

The colony's development was far from smooth. The Aborigines were not pleased to see the new arrivals, who promptly declared the land to be uninhabited and simply took it over. It is estimated that the population of Aborigines across Australia before 1770 was more than 300,000. They spoke 500 different languages that were as complex and rich as any European language, yet were dismissed as babble by the first settlers. The situation became worse for the Aborigines as they were thrown off their land, whole communities became infected by the foreign diseases that arrived along with the Europeans and some fell victim to imported social problems.

GOLD

The exploration of Australia came relatively late and progressed slowly. The inhospitable nature of much of the continent, the barrier of the Blue Mountains to the west of Sydney and the difficult nature of the Australian bush added to this slow development. It was the discovery of gold at Bathurst by Edward Hargraves in May 1851 that put Australia firmly on the map. This announcement sent shock waves around the world and the rush of prospectors to Bathurst from other colonies was so great that the population of Victoria declined rapidly. This was the first of many subsequent gold finds that attracted a flood of migrants to the Australian shores. Those miners who came initially for the gold remained as settlers and contributed their skills to the new land. This led to the rapid economic growth which made it possible for Australia to become relatively independent.

POST-WAR PEACE AND PROSPERITY

By 1880, Australia had a population of two million. By the end of World War I, that number had swelled to six million. After the end of World War II, the nation entered a boom time when there was a sustained period of rapid industrialisation and encouragement of immigration from Europe. The population then rose from seven million to eleven million with the influx of immigrants between 1945 and 1965. This wave saw the change of the culinary, psychological and cultural face of Australia. During this period when the population was increasing so dramatically the Australian government tried to influence the nationalities of the immigrants, by passing the Immigration Restriction Bill, known more commonly as the 'White Australian Policy'. This Bill had been introduced to prevent the immigration of Asian and Pacific Islander people, but was later revoked.

The number of Australians employed in the manufacturing industry had grown steadily since the beginning of the century, and many women who had taken over for the men while they were away at war were able to continue working during peacetime. Primary industries such as wheat and wool also continued to grow in output, although the percentage of Australians employed in the rural sector started to decline.

The economy developed strongly in the 1950s. This period saw the opening of mining resources and major nation-building projects like the huge hydro-electricity generator project in the Snowy Mountains. A prosperous society meant that everyone was benefiting, suburban property ownership increased and the government consolidated its political stability.

The establishment of a capital city for the country became a priority. The battle was bitterly fought out between Sydney and Melbourne, and the compromise meant that the government developed a new territory between the two cities on the Monaro Tablelands. Canberra was developed in 1913 as the head of the nation.

AN EVER-CHANGING SOCIETY

During the 1960s Australia's society and culture was again amidst the elements of change. The main reasons were the declining influence of Britain as a world power, the increasing domination of the United States especially during the Vietnam War and the increasing ethnic diversity within Australia's social make up. The 'Baby Boomers' had a huge effect on the nation's direction as their generation emerged as an active force behind a great deal of economic, political and social change.

In 1967 Australian citizens voted overwhelmingly in a national referendum to give the federal government the power to pass legislation on behalf of Australia's indigenous people. This showed an enormous amount of support towards improving the living conditions for both the Aboriginal and Torres Strait Islander communities by Australia as a whole. In 1993 a watershed was reached when the High Court rejected the view that Australia was unoccupied when the first fleet of settlers arrived. The

Court also recognised the right of Aborigines to claim sections of unoccupied land throughout the country. Although the Aborigines still remain Australia's most disadvantaged group the future is looking much brighter and increasingly harmonious.

The long post-war domination of the national political scene by the National Party finished in 1972 when the Labour Party won the general election. The following three years saw reforms and major legislative changes in education, health, social security, foreign affairs and industrial relations. However, in 1975 a constitutional crisis resulted in the Prime Minister, Gough Whitlam, being dismissed by the Governor General and subsequent defeat of the Labour party in the following election. The National Party dominated the political scene until 1983 when Labour once again came to office. The present coalition government, led by Prime Minister John Howard, took over from the Labour Party after winning the 1996 general election and was re-elected in 1998 and again in 2004.

(2)

Australia Today

Times have changed quite significantly and Australia's current immigration policies have become much more stringent. This has been driven purely by the fact that Australia has become an incredibly desirable place to live. The government now has much more discretion on who can enter, and so is now able to pick and choose from the applicants. This has come a long way from compulsory immigration during the early 1800s.

A STABLE DEMOCRACY

Australia has created a robust and pioneering democracy. The government structure reflects the British and North American models of liberal democracy, but at the same time has uniquely Australian features. The Commonwealth of Australia is a federation of six states and two self-governing territories. There are three tiers of government; all are democratically elected to office and are titled:

- Federal
- State
- Local.

The Federal Parliament, which sits in the national capital Canberra, consists of an Upper House called the Senate and a Lower House called the House of Representatives. The party (or parties) with the largest number of members

6

in the House of Representatives forms the government. The Senate acts mainly as a house of review.

Although Australia is an independent nation the British Head of State (currently Queen Elizabeth II) is still formally the Queen or King of Australia. The monarch appoints the Governor General, on the advice of the elected Australian government, to represent them. The Governor General appoints ministers on the advice of the Prime Minister and by convention acts on all matters of Parliament following the advice of the ministers. The power these governors exert is mainly ceremonial and there has been a lot of debate over whether Australia should become a republic.

Unlike Britain but similar to the United States of America, Australia has a written Constitution. This document sets out the functions of the Federal Government: mainly looking after the national economy, foreign policy and defence, social services and immigration. State and Territory Governments are run on similar lines to the Federal Government, but the leader of the Government is known as the Premier. They deal with all matters that are not assigned to the Federal Government: mainly education, health, transport and natural resources. In practice the two levels of government co-operate in many areas. The third tier is Local Government, which has responsibilities within the communities dealing with issues like urban and rural roads, rubbish removal and building codes.

Australia has full adult suffrage and voting is compulsory for all tiers of government. Although the fine for failing to vote is small, more than 90% of voters cast a ballot. In

recent times, Australia has effectively had a two-party
system at both State and Federal level, with the Australian
Labour Party and a coalition of the Liberal and National
Parties competing for power.

Australia's wealth, outward-looking policies and stability
have made this country important in world events. It is a
part of the Commonwealth of Nations, was a founding
member of the United Nations and was instrumental in
the founding of APEC.

THE ISLAND CONTINENT

Australia has often been referred to as the largest island
in the world and the smallest continent on earth, with an
area of 7.69 million square kilometres – to put this land
mass into perspective, you could fit the United Kingdom
into Australia just over 31 times. With such a vast land
area its geographical and climatic regions vary consider-
ably – from the tropics, rain forests and stunning
coastlines in the far north, to Australia's interior desert,
to the cooler more temperate mediterranean appearance
of the south coast, to the Alps in the east offering skiers
snow conditions to rival the best slopes in Europe.

Although Australia is the sixth largest nation after Russia,
Canada, China, the United States of America and Brazil,
it has a relatively small population, currently estimated at
19 million. Much of Australia is a plateau, bounded by
four seas and three oceans. It has an average elevation of
330 metres, which is the lowest of all the continents, with
its highest point being Mount Kosciuszko. However, what
Australia's landmasses lack in height they make up for in
variety. Visitors come from all around the world to see the

giant monolith Uluru (more commonly known as Ayers Rock), the vast Australian outback, the Great Barrier Reef and the stunning untouched coastlines.

STATES AND TERRITORIES
Australia's Federal Government, the six states and the two self-governing territories all share in the responsibility of governing the vast land area.

The Northern Territory
The Northern Territory has a lot to offer – a healthy lifestyle, modern infrastructure, a youthful and multicultural population and a dynamic economy. This territory has twice as much land area as France but a population of only 200,000. The Territory consists of a huge wilderness dotted with outposts of civilisation – mines, Aboriginal settlements, cattle stations and great national parks. The capital is Darwin, which was first established in 1869. Visitors come through this region to get to Alice Springs, Ayers Rock and the Kakadu national park. The region enjoys a very tropical climate but like most tropical destinations has been affected by the natural elements, most famously cyclone Tracey in 1974.

The Northern Territory exudes confidence. Significant industry sectors include tourism, mining, construction, agriculture, pastoral and horticulture. Darwin is the closest capital city to link with major Asian centres because of its geographical location, and the Northern Territory is forging ahead with business links as a result.

South Australia
South Australia was the first Australian state to be founded by the free settlers. It is a region famous for its

vineyards, award-winning wines and brandy. This state offers an exceptional lifestyle and a modern economy. The capital is Adelaide, which was designed by a British Army engineer called Colonel William in 1836. Most of South Australia's population lives in or near to Adelaide so travelling anywhere else gives the impression that you are in the real outback. South Australia has a strong case as a competitive, productive and creative location for business migrants. Adelaide is home to world class education and research facilities and backs innovation and technology. The South Australian government is working with potential investors to identify growth markets and potential partners. They have committed to fast track approval for new projects and businesses and are providing financial incentives and tailored support.

Australian Capital Territory
Canberra was established in 1911 as the site for the country's national capital. It is home to a number of institutes including the National Library, the National Gallery, the Australian War Memorial, the High Court and the Federal Parliament. Being the centre of the Australian government, administration and international affairs it has also become an extremely important centre for business. Canberra is home to 300,000 politicians, diplomats, public servants and academics amongst its growing population. As a completely planned city the national capital has few international rivals. It has been strategically placed in the southeast region between the busy markets of Melbourne and Sydney with a view to major growth and expansion. Originally designed by Walter Burley Griffin – an architect from Chicago – it has taken decades to complete. However, through the careful

planning Canberra has a very safe community environment and a cosmopolitan lifestyle; it has been able to combine modern city living with a clean environment.

Queensland

Better known as the Sunshine State, Queensland stretches from the tropical rain forests in the north, through the deserts to the Pacific coastline and is fringed by the Great Barrier Reef to the northeast. A state of extremes means that you can find everything from cosmopolitan cities to a slower pace of life in small towns and settlements. Brisbane is the capital, rising from penal beginnings to become Australia's third largest city. Queensland's population currently stands at 3.5 million, of which just over 1.5 million live in Brisbane. There is a huge pull towards this city purely because of the quality of life. The attractions include beaches, islands, beautiful weather, fresh yet cheap food, easy to use transport and business opportunities.

In Australia's fastest growing state the economic activity and growth is in tourism, manufacturing, technology, primary industry and services.

Tasmania

Tasmania is an island found 300km off the south eastern tip of Australia. It is separated from the continent by the Bass Strait and is a beautiful, temperate, green island that has remained largely unspoilt and unpolluted. The island has an enormous amount of forests, mountains and fertile farmlands that have been protected as reserves and national parks. Hobart is Tasmania's capital and is Australia's second oldest city after Sydney. It is located at the bottom of the island and has been made famous in recent years by the Sydney to Hobart yacht race that takes place every year on New Year's Day. Tasmania produces some of the world's finest wool and food products, and sells advanced technology products to more than 40 niche markets.

Victoria

Victoria is the smallest of the mainland states. Of its population of close to 4.5 million people, 3 million live in the capital city of Melbourne. The colony of Victoria was originally settled by gold miners around the Ballarat and Bendigo region, farmers and herders in the Murray and Goulburn valleys and whalers and sealers at Apollo Bay and Port Fairy. Melbourne is Australia's second largest city and was established in 1835. It is an incredibly popular city to live in. Geographically it sits at the bottom of Australia on the coast. It experiences a mixture of temperature extremes and definitely sees each of the four seasons – sometimes in one day! The city is a wonderful place to live, with a medley of gardens, culture, beautiful architecture, arts, fashion and a growing business economy.

Western Australia

Western Australia is a huge and empty state. It is about the size of Western Europe, with almost three quarters of the state's population of 2 million people living in its capital Perth. Perth is separated from the rest of Australia by the barren expanse of the Nullarbor Plain and is therefore geographically the most remote city in the world. Much of Western Australia's wealth is based in large mining and mineral companies, while other flourishing industries include manufacturing, tourism and primary industries. Migrants moving to Perth enjoy a near perfect climate, alongside a mediterranean lifestyle, clean air and a very low cost of living. The city is close to beautiful beaches and rivers so you don't have far to go to get out of the cosmopolitan world.

New South Wales

With almost 6 million people, New South Wales is Australia's most popular state. Sydney is where it all started in 1788 when the first British fleet landed on its shores. It has since become the international gateway for millions of tourists each year to start their travels before moving on to experience the rest of Australia. Sydney is home to more than 4 million people and is definitely Australia's best known city. It is renowned not only for its great beauty but also for its world famous buildings such as the Sydney Harbour Bridge and the Opera House. Sydney has all the benefits of a large city: it is exciting, busy, beautiful and cultural yet this is crossed with the laid back attitude of the locals.

In September 2000 the eyes of the world were focused on Sydney as it played host to the games of the XXVII Olympiad. The games were a tremendous success for Australia as 3.5 billion people from around the world watched one of the most celebrated games to date. The total economic benefit to Australia was estimated at over 6 billion dollars, with over 15,000 media representatives covering the event. These games cemented the view that Sydney is one of the most beautiful and modern cities in the world today.

The city is open and spacious and is surrounded on three sides by national parks, the fourth side being lined with a spectacular 60km coastline. The 'Sydneysiders', it is said, live magnificently by world standards. They inhabit the areas from the harbour out to the beaches and far flung suburbs, choosing between the faster city lights and the quieter and more relaxed suburban lifestyles.

On top of the social and lifestyle aspect, Sydney is also known to be home to Australia's most influential central business district, as most national and international offices choose to have their major Australian companies in the city. As a result Sydney has become an attractive place to live with opportunities and lifestyle choices for a broad spectrum of people.

3

Education in Australia

THE EDUCATION SYSTEM

Education standards in Australia are amongst the highest in the world, and Federal and State Governments have ensured that these standards are regulated and maintained. The Federal Department of Employment, Education and Training (DEET) is the main government body responsible for the overall education policies, ensuring that there is a consistency of standards throughout Australia.

Access to quality education has always been seen by Australians as part of their child's birthright and community involvement in monitoring the standard of education is very high.

The education system is broken up into five separate areas:

- preschooling/daycare/playgroup
- infants and primary school
- secondary school
- career and vocational training
- university.

Minimising any educational differences between states and territories ensures that students across the country have complied equally with the standards required for entry into tertiary education. There is the option within the education system to have your child enrol with a public or private school. The difference is that the public school system is owned by the government and is free to everyone (although there is a fee to cover yearly extra curricular activities) and the private schools are run by an independent body with annual fees being charged by the school. Currently up to 35% of children are enrolled at private schools throughout Australia, and early registration of your child at these schools is recommended as competition is strong and waiting lists are getting longer.

PRESCHOOLING/DAYCARE/PLAYGROUP
The starting age for these schools is three years old and although none of these schools are compulsory, many children start their education in one form or another at one of the above mentioned centres. As these are privately owned, early registration is advisable, as places are limited.

INFANT AND PRIMARY SCHOOL
Children in infant and primary schools are grouped together on the basis of their age and development level. The progression to the following year is based on an evaluation of the student's development during the year. Most schools have a uniform for the pupils to wear and this now includes a hat, because of the strength of the sun in Australia. Research has shown that long-term exposure to the sun has harsh effects and can cause damage, and as a result most schools now have the policy 'no hat – no play'.

Public schools tend to be co-educational, while private schools have a higher proportion of single sex environments. Private schools also offer a more diverse range of specialist subjects like computing studies, science and music at this age. Public schools do, however, teach a mixture of languages through a syllabus called 'LOTE' – Language Other Than English.

SECONDARY SCHOOL

Secondary school is only compulsory up to the age of 15. There are two more years of schooling after this age and the majority of students do tend to stay on throughout the entire education system. English, science and maths are compulsory during the first couple of years, but there is a broad range of elective subjects that the students can choose from to fill out their timetable. As the students progress through the school system, teachers actively encourage them to talk through subject options and career directions with a career advisor, especially as universities do require specific papers to be completed before entry is permitted onto specific courses.

Supplementary education is offered if the course that the student wants to enrol on conflicts with other papers, or is not currently on offer at their school. This will come in the form either of correspondence papers or school on Saturday. All registered courses of study at secondary school are accredited by the relevant state (or territory) authorities. Completing the final year of study, however, does not entitle the student to immediate entry onto the university course of their choice. Places on Tertiary courses are limited and competition is strong.

International Baccalaureate is a programme with a high international profile and is offered during the last few years of school. This course allows the student to gain entry to a number of overseas universities and gain advanced placement in some American universities.

CAREER AND VOCATIONAL TRAINING

There are again both public and private education services provided in this sector:

◆ TAFE – Technical and Further Education – is regulated by the government,

◆ ACPET is the Australian Council of Private Education and Training.

These courses have a strong and practical focus towards the career that the student is aiming for. Fees are charged for these courses but the costs vary between courses, tertiary institutes and states. Most courses offer a Diploma or Associate Diploma level and few are offered as degrees.

UNIVERSITY

The Australian universities prepare students for entry into specific professions. There is an emphasis on both teaching and research so that a full range of both academic and professional disciplines can be offered with awards ranging from an Associate Diploma to a Doctorate. Most universities have a multi-campus structure with each campus specialising in a particular discipline – they act as separate departments which then link back to the main campus. Some universities offer residential accommodation on site and a series of external clubs and extra-curricular activities to complete the student lifestyle.

4

Health Care Services in Australia

THE PUBLIC HEALTH CARE SYSTEM

Australians are served by one of the most comprehensive and highest quality health care systems in the world. This public health care system was established in 1984 and is known as Medicare.

Through Medicare, Australians have the assurance of knowing that they have access to free public hospital treatment and free or subsidised medical care and that this service is available to everyone regardless of income, age or health status.

Medicare also provides both free hospital and medical cover for permanent residents who are financially disadvantaged such as low income earners and those receiving benefits from the government such as sickness benefit, unemployment benefit, aged pension and invalid pension.

Treatment and admission to a public hospital is guaranteed for emergencies such as accidents, heart attacks or urgent surgery. Minor or less acute illnesses can also be treated within the public hospital system. Be aware, however, that due to the high demand for treatments on this public service, there are lengthy waiting lists for elective surgery, which means that you will not be able to specify a time or date on which you would like your treatment to take place.

PRIVATE HEALTH INSURANCE

Private health insurance is available to anyone wanting to cover the costs of becoming a private patient. The benefits of becoming a private patient are:

◆ You choose your treating doctor.

◆ You may reduce the waiting time for your elective surgery.

◆ It provides cover for other services that are not covered by Medicare including dental, optical, pharmaceutical, physiotherapy and a wide range of other services.

Around 34% of Australians choose to take out private health insurance, and 24% have taken it out with a company called Medicare Private. This is just one insurance company that you can take cover with, but the main advantage of Medicare Private is that they are able to offer hospital insurance that covers 100% of hospital charges including extra costs like telephone calls, television rental and newspapers.

Private health funds are regulated by the Commonwealth Government, and all follow the principle of community rating. This means that everyone pays the same – the premiums charged by funds do not vary according to age, sex, state of health or the size of your family. So a family premium will be double that of a single premium regardless of how many family members there are, and a young healthy single person will pay the same as an elderly, unwell single person provided they have taken out the same cover.

Rules regarding membership vary between funds and between states, so it is a good idea to ring around and do some research on what is on offer and what cover suits you best within the area that you decide to settle in. Health insurance does provide options for those who want the comfort and convenience of treatment in a private hospital.

WHERE TO GO IF YOU GET SICK

If you or your family get sick the first port of call will most likely be your local doctor, a General Practitioner (GP). If your condition or illness requires further attention then your GP will advise you to see a specialist.

Although the visit to your GP or specialist is not free, a rebate through Medicare is available. This rebate is 85% of the Medical Benefits Schedule (MBS) fee. The MBS sets down fees for services determined by the government to be fair to both patient and doctor. Low income earners and those receiving benefits will receive a 'Health Care Card'. Holders of this card do not pay anything for a visit to the doctor, as the GP will directly bill Medicare for the rebate.

The Commonwealth Government also subsidises most prescription medications brought at pharmacies through a scheme called the Pharmaceutical Benefits Scheme. This provides access to prescription medication at a reasonable cost. Health Care Card holders pay a low set fee per prescription.

If you are being admitted to a public hospital then you should have your Medicare card with you. If you want to be admitted as a public patient (even if you have private health insurance) then you can be, but they will need the details of your Medicare card. The only costs you should pay as a public patient at a public hospital are any extras like television or phone services. Medicare covers all of the hospital and medical charges.

If you hold private health insurance then more than likely your doctor will make the booking for you. You will be required to fill out forms regarding your medical history and personal details, and you may even need to attend pre-admission blood tests and X-rays. If you do not have 100% coverage you will be asked to pay the difference as you leave. If you do not have health insurance you will be asked to pay the anticipated costs before you are admitted.

(5)

Enjoying Australia

Australia's climate and geography provide the perfect playground for relaxation and enjoyment for the entire family. Almost every leisure pursuit known to man can be found within the Australia boundaries. From snowy mountains to the deep blue sea, this is the ultimate environment to satisfy your sporting and leisure requirements all year round.

BOATING

The large expanse of water surrounding Australia, the ideal weather, the plentiful and secure anchorages and the abundant inland waterway systems are more than enough to entice the majority of Australia's population to spend at lot of their time around, in and on the water. Australia has been renowned as a nation of 'boaties' and 'yachties' for years and boat ownership is very popular, with facilities for all classes ranging from dinghies to multi-million-dollar yachts and cruisers. Registration of all boats that are capable of doing 10 knots or more is compulsory and the drivers are required to hold a general boating licence and have a thorough knowledge of local rules and conditions. The Boating Industry Association is represented in most states; they are there to offer advice and assistance in the purchase and ownership of all types of boats.

GOLF

Australia has over 1,000 golf courses around the country and a large number are world class, designed to test both the casual and more serious players. The ranges are often situated in beautiful locations. The Cypress Lakes and Country Club is located in the Hunter Valley 130kms north of Sydney – this is not only a demanding course but has the added advantage of being situated right in the heart of the Hunter Valley wine district. This golf range, like many others, provides a pleasant backdrop to both social and business activities. Some courses are incorporated in resorts and accept casual players only, while others are more established members-only clubs, which do not accept any new members, although there are also a number of newer clubs with top courses which are actively pursuing new membership.

MOTORING

Australia is one of the most motorised countries in the world. Because of the distances between work, home and social events, people rely on their cars to get them around. Many people take advantage of the good quality roads and highways and get out into the wide open space that is so much part of Australia. Many clubs have been set up and information on these will be at your local community council or information office.

FISHING

Fishing is the most popular leisure activity in Australia, which is not surprising given the country's vast coastline and inland waterways. Some of the best sea fishing does not even require a boat – you can fish off the beaches and rocks in your local area and still find a wide range of fish. The ultimate ocean fish is the black marlin, which can grow beyond 700kg and is renowned in the fishing world as a great fighting fish. Trout fishing is generally restricted to the Snowy Mountain region in New South Wales, with popular brown, brook and rainbow trout found in these rivers. The Murray River cod is any freshwater fisherman's dream; specimens as large as 1.8 metres long, weighing over 100kg have been caught.

HORSE RACING

Racing is very much part of the Australian psyche, and there is a great range of opportunities to be involved in this sport, from being an owner of a thoroughbred horse, to having a punt at the local race course. The once-a-year, nation stopping Melbourne Cup has become increasingly popular and now draws horses from as far away as Ireland. This event is held in November and has become a folk festival as much as it is a fiercely competitive horse race. Australians are amongst the greatest gamblers on earth with the turnover climbing to well over A$7 billion a year from the TAB. A percentage of this money is now being returned to race clubs as prize money or to improve facilities for both the public going to the races and the horses.

OTHER SPORTS

Australia is a sporting nation. Not only do Australians play sport, but they watch sport, bet on sport and talk sport probably more than anything else. The climate, natural opportunities and adequate leisure time all provide the perfect framework for any sporting activities. There are only a few countries in the world where you can take part in such a variety of sports and with such ease over the entire year. There is a large number of sporting clubs and teams available, from community based projects, business social teams, club sports through to professionals. If sport is your thing then you will be able to find something that fits into your schedule in the sport that you like.

Popular sports include soccer, rugby, Aussie rules football, golf, tennis, bowls, basketball, netball and athletics, just to name a few. The mountains of New South Wales, Tasmania and Victoria offer horse treks in the summer and skiing in the winter. The beaches all around Australia offer surfing, windsurfing, swimming, scuba diving, and the rivers and harbours join in with more places to sail and waterski. Jogging and walking are national pastimes, all the major cities have beautiful gardens for you to experience and there are great tracks and walkways through the mountainous and coastal areas as well.

ARTS

Australia has drawn its population from more than 120 countries from around the world, and its culture and arts reflect this vast resource. Australia's cultural life is rich and diverse. It looks into the past and works its magic into the present.

There are museums all over the country that focus on Australia's maritime, technology, culture and natural history. These museums offer experiences that take you from the beginning of time to the local area. Capital cities all boast an abundance of art galleries, holding some of the finest Australian and overseas paintings and sculptures. The Australian Ballet and Theatre Companies are famous not only within the country but on an international scale. They tour regularly to other major world cities and festivals. Australia has also produced a number of outstanding opera and pop singers, as well as rock and mainstream bands.

6

Staying in Australia Temporarily

People holidaying in Australia must seek a visitor visa (tourist class) from the Australian High Commission. Australia offers visitors a visitor visa that lasts three months or one that lasts for six months. If you are issued with a three month visa the holder must enter within 12 months from the date of issue. However, if you receive a six month visa then the holder may enter within four years from the date of issue, or before the passport expires, whichever occurs first. Australia has very strict rules on overstaying so it is vital that applicants do not fall into an overstay situation.

All people applying for a temporary residence visa must meet health and character criteria. In line with this some applicants my need to undergo a medical and chest X-ray before approval is given.

A person on a temporary residence visa will normally be allowed to travel out of and re-enter Australia for the duration of their visa. It is worth noting that people who stay in the country past the expiry of their visa seriously jeopardise their right to future visits or migration plans.

TAKING A HOLIDAY

Australia offers a wide range of visa categories to enable you to stay in the country on a temporary basis. Over the 1997–98 financial year almost 100,000 temporary visas were granted to overseas citizens.

Temporary residents with the right to work must pay taxes on any income earned in Australia. They will normally be prevented from claiming social welfare benefits or national public health cover unless they come from a country that has a Reciprocal Health Care Agreement with the Australian government.

USING THE WORKING HOLIDAY SCHEME

The working holiday scheme encourages an international understanding between countries. It provides opportunities for young people to experience Australia through travel and holidaying, and allows them limited work opportunities.

Australia has reciprocal arrangements with the United Kingdom, Canada, the Netherlands, Japan, the Republic of Ireland, the Republic of Korea, Malta, Germany, Denmark, Sweden, Norway, the Hong Kong Special Administrative Region of the People's Republic of China, Finland and the Republic of Cyprus. Young people from other countries may apply providing they can show the benefits that would be gained in granting them the visa.

Applicants must show that:

◆ They are between the ages of 18 and 25 years and have no dependants. Citizens up to 30 years of age may apply if they are from countries that have a reciprocal scheme with Australia.

- The main reason to travel to Australia is for a holiday, and that any work taken will be incidental to support themselves while holidaying.

- They will not enrol to study, apart from short-term English language courses.

- They will leave Australia at the end of their authorised stay.

CATEGORIES FOR TEMPORARY IMMIGRATION

Retirement category

Qualifying retirees may live in Australia for a period of four years. Further extensions of two years may be gained if the applicant still meets the requirements for the issuing of the visa.

The requirements for the visa are:

- Be at least 55 years of age.

- Have no dependants other than a spouse or de facto partner.

- Meet the health and character requirements.

- Have capital of A$870,000 to transfer to Australia (or A$800,000 if they have a non-dependant child living permanently in Australia) or

- Have capital of A$350,000 to transfer plus a yearly income of at least A$52,000 from a pension or capital (or A$315,000 plus other income of A$50,000 if they have a non-dependent child living permanently in Australia).

Retirement visas now include limited work rights which will allow the holder to work for a maximum of 20 hours per week.

Emergency category

This allows applicants who have applied for a temporary residency visa, but are awaiting approval on the health and character criteria, the right to travel to Australia if they can demonstrate an urgent need to do so.

Confirmatory category

This approves the stay of people who have entered Australia on an emergency visa once their outstanding health and character checks have been met.

Exchange category

This allows citizens from countries that have reciprocal arrangements to enter Australia.

Foreign government agency category

Employees of foreign governments which have no official status, or those officials who do not have diplomatic or official status, have the right to stay in Australia on the basis of carrying out official business.

Special programme

This allows Churchill Fellows or other approved community based non-commercial programme members the chance to enter Australia to develop international relations.

Visiting academic category
People who have been invited by an Australian research or tertiary institute may travel to Australia to observe and participate (without payment) in projects.

Entertainment category
This grants entry for performers and their supporters who will be involved with the Australian entertainment industry.

Sport category
This allows sportspeople, sporting officials and support staff to engage in competitions and training in Australia.

Media and film category
Professional media and support staff may seek entry under this category.

Public lecturer category
This enables professional lecturers and recognised experts to take up invitations to make public presentations.

Family relationship category
This provides the opportunity of an extended holiday for young people under the age of 18 to stay with relatives or close family friends in Australia.

Domestic worker/diplomatic or consular
This allows entry for domestic workers and official staff in Australia. This application must be supported by the Australian Department of Foreign Affairs and Trade.

Religious worker

This allows religious and evangelical workers to serve the spiritual needs of their faith in Australia.

Supported dependant (of an Australian or New Zealand citizen)

This allows for dependant family members of Australian citizens, permanent residents and eligible New Zealand citizens temporary residence in Australia.

Expatriate category

This gives the right of temporary residence to the dependants of expatriate employees stationed in isolated locations in Papua New Guinea, the South Pacific and southeast Asia.

Diplomatic category

This gives approval for diplomats, consular officials and employees and certain members of specialist United Nations agencies temporary entry into Australia.

SKILLED INDEPENDENT REGIONAL CATEGORY (TEMPORARY)

The Skilled Independent Regional (SIR) visa has been developed in consultation with the State/Territory governments. The main aim of the SIR visa is to assist in the development of regional Australia through skilled migration. The SIR visa allows an initial stay of three years during which time the SIR visa holder must live and work in their chosen area of regional Australia or a low growth metropolitan area.

At the date of writing these areas are as follows:

Regional Australia/low population growth metropolitan areas	Postcodes inclusive
New South Wales except Sydney, Newcastle, the Central Coast and Wollongong	2311 to 2312 2328 to 2333 2340 to 2411 2428 to 2490 2536 to 2551 2575 to 2594 2618 to 2739 2787 to 2898
Queensland except Brisbane metropolitan area and the Gold Coast	4301 to 4899
Victoria except Melbourne metropolitan area	3139 3212 to 3334 3340 to 3424 3430 to 3649 3658 to 3749 3753, 3756, 3758, 3762, 3764 3778 to 3781 3783, 3797, 3799 3810 to 3909 3921 to 3925 3945 to 3974 3979 3981 to 3996
Western Australia except Perth metropolitan area	6041 to 6044 6121 to 6126 6200 to 6799
South Australia	entire state
Tasmania	entire state
Northern Territory	entire territory

Note: none of the Australian Capital Territory is included.

Once you have lived in regional Australia or a low growth metropolitan area for at least two years and are able to show evidence that you have been employed for a minimum of 12 months, you are eligible to apply for permanent residence through a range of existing categories of regional visa. These include the Regional Sponsored Migration Scheme (RSMS), State/Territory Nominated Independent (STNI) or the Sponsored Business Owner category (details can be found in Chapters 7 and 8).

You are able to apply for an SIR visa in the following circumstances:

♦ You are outside Australia and meet the basic requirements (see below).

♦ You are outside Australia and have already lodged a General Skilled Migration application which has been pooled, and you meet the SIR passmark of 110.

♦ You are already in Australia on an eligible student visa, and you meet the basic requirements (see below).

Basic requirements
To be eligible to apply for an SIR visa you must meet the following criteria:

♦ Be under 45 years of age at the time of application.

♦ Have an occupation that is listed on the skilled occupations list. Please refer to the Glossary, where a detailed version of this document is listed.

- Have obtained a successful outcome of your skills assessment from the relevant assessing authority in Australia (information can be found in Chapter 4).

- Have at least 12 to 24 months' recent work experience depending on your occupation.

- Hold sponsorship from a relevant State/Territory authority.

Sponsorship

All applicants are required to hold sponsorship from an appropriate authority of a State/Territory government. The approved sponsorship form 1224 must be lodged with the application form 47SK.

Each State/Territory government has their own sponsorship guidelines in line with their own particular employment and economic needs. Information pertaining to employment, housing, schools and other services in the regions in which you are interested can be found at *www.immi.gov.au/migration/skilled/sir.htm*

SIR applicants must be aware that sponsorship by a State/Territory government does **not** mean:

- Your SIR visa will be automatically granted. Applicants will be assessed against the legal requirement in place and only if all criteria are met will a visa be granted.

- Employment will be arranged by the relevant State/Territory government who sponsors you. Individuals should make every effort to contact potential employers and arrange interviews in their chosen location.

◆ You will be granted permanent residency at the expiry of your visa. To apply for permanent residency you must have abided by all conditions of your SIR visa and lodge an application under one of the following categories:
  – Regional Sponsored Migration Scheme (RSMS)
  – State/Territory Nominated Independent (STNI)
  – Sponsored Business Owner category.

Details of theses categories can be found in Chapters 7 and 8.

(7)

Staying in Australia Permanently

In the post World War II era Australia set up a large scale migration programme in agreement with the British, other European and the International Refugee Organisation to encourage migration, especially from war-torn Europe.

Since that time the migration programme has undergone many changes, revisions and updates to take into account the changing needs of the Australian economy and society. This migration programme has seen 5.7 million people settle in Australia and the population rise from 7 million to 18.6 million. Successive governments have modified and developed policy around the needs of the country, the people and the economy.

Today Australia is one of the few countries in the world to run a permanent migration programme to actively encourage potential migrants to settle in the country. The policy is non-discriminatory and means that anyone from any country can apply to migrate regardless of their gender, ethnic origin or religion.

MIGRATION PROGRAMME

In broad terms the immigration programme can be split into the following categories:

Family stream

This allows people with family links to Australian citizens or permanent residence the right to live and work in Australia.

Skilled stream

This seeks to bring in people with business or work skills or other special talents that would be of benefit to Australia's economic growth.

The government hoped to attract 100,000 immigrants for 2004/2005 places on the permanent migration programme, with roughly half going to people with family links in Australia, the remainder having business or professional skills and abilities. There is also a humanitarian programme for refugees and displaced people who have suffered human rights violations or discrimination.

The major reasons for migrating are for family reunion, cultural change, economic and career opportunities, political stability and the appeal of the lifestyle and environment.

Eligibility under the skilled stream

Australia's permanent migration programme encourages people with professional or trade occupations to settle in Australia. More than half of the 100,000 places on the migration programme are allocated to skilled migrants.

You may apply if you :

- Are under 45 years of age at the time of application.

- Have an occupation that is listed on the Skilled Occupations List. Please refer page 161 for a detailed version of this document.

- Have obtained a successful outcome of your skills assessment from the relevant assessing authority in Australia.

- Have at least 12 to 24 months' recent work experience depending on your occupation.

IDENTIFYING YOUR OCCUPATION

There are over 400 specific jobs listed on the Skilled Occupations List (SOL) that may qualify a person for permanent migration to Australia. You will need to confirm that you have an occupation that is on this list.

The list is grouped into four major categories:

- managers and administrators
- professionals
- associate professionals
- tradepersons and related workers.

It is important to ensure that the occupation that is chosen from the list accurately reflects your experience. Occupations and job titles often differ from country to country, and may be known by a different name in Australia.

Many of the job titles on the list cover a wide range of roles and specialisations. If you need to clarify what occupation would be best for you to apply under you should either contact the relevant assessing authority, or browse through the Australian Standard Classification of Occupations book (ASCO).

The Skilled Occupations List also shows:

♦ the ASCO number for the occupation
♦ the relevant assessing authority for the occupation
♦ the number of points allocated for the occupation points test.

GETTING YOUR SKILLS ASSESSED

Before a full migration application can be submitted, the candidate's qualifications, skills, experience and competence in their chosen occupation must be assessed by the relevant assessing authority in Australia. The purpose of this assessment is to ensure that the person is suitably trained, qualified and experienced to work in the nominated occupation. The government relies on trade associations and professional societies to assess applicants' skills.

The benefit of the skills assessment is that it will help the candidate determine whether it will be worthwhile to submit a full application. In the past many people went through the effort of preparing a full migration application only to find at the last stages that they did not meet the Australian standards for their occupation, and therefore could not be approved for permanent migration.

Each authority has different procedures to assess a candidate's skills, but in general they will want to see evidence of tertiary or trade qualifications, and proof of any relevant work experience. They will contact the specific authority that deals with your nominated occupation for exact details on how to have your skills assessed. Included below is a general list of information and documentation that the majority of assessing authorities ask for:

Identification
- Copy of full-length birth certificate, or
- copy of identification pages of passport
- evidence of change of name (if applicable, e.g., marriage certificate)
- two passport photographs.

Education
- Copies of all post secondary qualifications and certificates (e.g. degree, diploma).

- Transcripts of courses completed, including details of the duration, date of completion and subjects covered and evidence of the nature and content of the training, describing the content of each subject studied for the machines, tools and equipment on which you were trained.

- Registration or licensing membership.

- Any documentation not in English must be accompanied by an English translation from a certified translator.

Work experience/employment history

In further support of your application, you will need to provide evidence of all your previous and current employment. This should be submitted in the form of a statement of service/reference on company letterhead and signed by a company official. The statement should include the following:

◆ Exact dates when your employment with each specific company commenced and terminated and details of training undertaken and any promotions.

◆ The position/classification in which you were employed.

◆ A full and detailed description of the nature and content of your work tasks and the tools and equipment used.

Where applicable also provide:

◆ Evidence of trade training undertaken during service in the armed forces, e.g. training and employment record (if applicable).

If references for each period of employment are not available (e.g. the company has gone out of business), please provide:

◆ certified copies of your annual tax returns
◆ pay advice/wage slips
◆ job specifications
◆ letters of appointment.

Self-employment

If you have been self-employed at any time you should provide the following:

- A personal statement on a properly signed statutory declaration, affidavit or similar legal declaration (with your signature witnessed by a legal authority in your country) providing full details on:
  - the exact commencement and completion date of each period of self-employment
  - the occupations in which you were self-employed
  - the nature and content of the work tasks you personally performed
  - the number of staff employed and their occupations
  - your workshop and the tools and equipment used
  - your business registration certificate.

- At least three statements from suppliers, on letterhead paper, confirming the nature of business, trading dates, the total amount of all material/equipment purchased over a 12-month period and the types of material equipment supplied.

- At least three statements from clients, on letterhead paper, with full details of the work you did for them including dates and the total amount of contracts executed over a 12-month period.

- A statement on letterhead paper from your accountant or legal representative certifying the name and nature of your business, the exact dates of the period of self-employment and the capacity in which you have been self-employed.

PAYMENT OF FEES

All the assessing authorities in Australia charge a fee to carry out a skills assessment. These range from approximately A$100 to A$1000 depending on the occupation. While a few assessing authorities accept credit cards most of them will require the money in the form of a bank draft or money order. This will need to be drawn on an Australian bank that will clear in Australia. You will also need to check with the assessing authority who to make the cheque payable to.

HOW TO HAVE YOUR DOCUMENTS CORRECTLY CERTIFIED

This is the stage where many people encounter problems with their applications. While the following procedures may seem long-winded and pedantic, they are put in place by the assessing authorities to ensure that the information they are receiving is true and factual.

♦ **All** documentation submitted to the assessing authority **must** be certified copies of the originals.

Accordingly, you are required to make photocopies of documents and then take these photocopies, along with the originals, to a person authorised by the Australian government to certify documents. This authorised person will compare the copies with the originals and certify (in the appropriate words) on the copy itself that the photocopy is a true copy of the original document. Failure to adhere to these procedures will render your application invalid, and it will be returned to you, possibly a number of months later, asking you to resubmit it in the correct format.

A list of persons authorised to certify photocopied documents

1. Solicitor/barrister
2. Justice of the Peace/magistrate
3. Notary public
4. Commissioner for oaths/affidavits

What each certified photocopy must bear

◆ The full name of the authorised person
◆ The person's status, e.g. solicitor, GP
◆ The person's signature
◆ The person's official stamp or seal.

You should not send a photocopy of a document where the certification itself is also part of the photocopy. The certification must always be put onto the photocopied document.

Although the approved person may charge you for this certification service, you should always adhere to the above list of approved persons, as other persons will not be considered acceptable and this will result in your application being returned to you without being processed.

THE APPLICATION PROCESS

How long will it take?

Processing times vary depending on agency procedures and the case load they have to deal with. Average processing times may range from two to six months, though agencies will normally issue a letter confirming receipt of the application once they have received it. If the assessing authority requires further information they will normally ask for this by way of a letter. This further information should be promptly forwarded to them to allow them to reach a decision on the case as quickly as possible.

What can I expect the result to be?

If the assessing authority feels that you meet the requirements they will respond with a confirmation letter. They will also give a recommendation on the points that you should be awarded in support of your migration application, though it should be noted that the final decision on occupation points lies with the Department of Immigration and Multicultural and Indigenous Affairs (DIMIA) processing case officer. For occupations that require Australian registration they may also provide details of any extra registration requirements that will need to be undertaken. This could include conversion courses and/or professional training.

If the assessing authority feels that you do not meet the required standards they will normally provide you with guidance on what will need to be done for their criteria to be met. This might be a period of further work experience or extra studies to gain the necessary qualifications. If the skills assessment was positive the next step will be to clarify what the work experience requirements are for your application.

CLARIFYING YOUR WORK EXPERIENCE

- If your nominated occupation is worth 60 points you must have been in paid employment in the skilled occupations for at least 12 out of the last 18 months before submitting your full migration application.

- If your nominated occupation is worth 40 or 50 points, you must have been in paid employment in a skilled occupation for at least two out of the past three years before applying.

♦ If you are applying under the skills matching or skilled regional sponsored categories you may be eligible with less work experience.

♦ You will be exempt from the work experience requirements if you have completed an Australian qualification within the six months before submitting your full migration application. This six-month period begins from the date of the completed qualification, and not from the date the qualification was conferred.

Tip

Many people applying for a permanent migration visa may not have worked in their nominated occupation for a number of years, and so would not be able to meet the work experience requirements. What some people opt to do is to have their skills assessed, and if the result of this is positive they take employment in their nominated occupation to gain the necessary work experience. After gaining the required experience they can then submit their full migration application.

THE POINTS TEST

There are two categories that require you to pass a points test to be eligible for permanent migration to Australia. They are:

1. Skilled – Australian sponsored
2. Skilled – independent.

Points are awarded for:

◆ skills
◆ age
◆ English language ability
◆ specific work experience
◆ occupation in demand (or a job offer)
◆ Australian qualifications
◆ spouse skills
◆ relationship (skilled – Australian sponsored/designated area sponsored only).

Extra points will be awarded for capital investment in Australia, Australian skilled work experience, or fluency in one of Australia's major community languages.

The pass mark and pool mark

There are two separate score marks on the permanent migration scheme. You must have enough points to meet or exceed the pass mark. The pass mark is taken as the one that is in effect at the time your application is assessed, not when your application was lodged.

The second mark is the pool mark. If your points score does not reach the pass mark, but meets or exceeds the pool mark, your application will be held by the DIMIA for up to two years. If over the two-year period the pass mark is lowered and your points score meets or exceeds the new pass mark, your case will be processed further.

The present pass mark and pool mark scores are listed below.

	Pass mark	Pool mark
Skilled – Australian sponsored category	110	105
Skilled – independent category	120	70

Skills

The occupation you nominate affects how your skills qualifications are assessed. The occupation must be on the Skilled Occupations List at the time you apply. If the assessing authority deems your skills are suitable for the occupation you will normally be awarded the allocated points mark from the skilled occupations list.

60 points will be awarded to most occupations where training is specific to that occupation. You will normally need to have a degree or trade certificate qualification as well as experience in your nominated occupation as well as meeting the registration requirements in Australia. For some occupations work experience will be taken in lieu of formal qualifications.

50 points will be given for more general professional occupations. A qualification equivalent to an Australian degree is normally required, though it does not need to be specific to your nominated occupation.

40 points – other general skilled occupations. These occupations will require the qualification equivalent to an Australian advanced diploma, though they do not need to be specific to the nominated occupation.

Age

Age at time of application	Points
18 – 29	30
30 – 34	25
35 – 39	20
40 – 44	15

You will need to provide a certified copy of your birth certificate as proof of your age.

English language ability

English language ability	IELTS Standard	Points
Vocational English Applicants must have reasonable command of English language, and be able to cope with overall meaning in most situations. They must be able to communicate effectively in their area of employment.	IELTS score of at least five on each of the four components in the test – speaking, reading, writing and listening.	15
Competent English Applicants must have an effective command of English language. They must be able to use and understand complex sentences.	IELTS score of at least six on each of the four components in the test – speaking, reading, writing and listening.	20

All applicants are encouraged to obtain proof of their English language ability.

There are a number of methods of doing this:

♦ Provide evidence that you are a native English speaker – which will award you points for competent English. If you were born and raised in an English speaking country you will normally be awarded points for having competent English.

If you were not born and raised in an English speaking country you may need to provide the following proof:

♦ That you have undertaken post secondary studies at an institution where the instruction was in English.

♦ Undertake an International English Language Testing System (IELTS) test. You will normally only need to take the general training test, unless you are advised otherwise by your skills assessing authority. These test results will remain valid for 12 months.

♦ Points for competent English will also be awarded for a pass in the occupational English test or equivalent. This will normally be taken on the advice from your assessing authority

If DIMIA has any doubts about your English language ability they may ask you to take an IELTS test if one has not been done already.

Specific work experience

	Points
If your nominated occupation is worth 60 points and you have worked in that occupation, or a closely related occupation, for at least three out of the four years before you apply.	10
If your nominated occupation is worth 40, 50 or 60 points, and you have worked in skilled employment (any of the occupations on the skilled list) for at least three out of the four years before you apply.	5

To gain points for specific work experience you need to obtain proof by way of employment references and detailed duty statements covering the required period. These may be the same documents that you provide to meet the recent work experience requirements.

Occupation in demand or job offer

There are a number of occupations that are in acute demand in Australia. To encourage people with these skills to apply for permanent migration, the DIMIA awards extra points for these occupations. They are also willing to offer further points if the applicant has a job offer in that nominated occupation with an organisation that has employed at least ten people on a full-time basis for the previous two financial years.

	Points
Occupation in demand, but no job offer	15
Occupation in demand with job offer	20

Points will only be awarded if the nominated occupation is on the Migration Occupations in Demand List (MODL) at the time when the application is assessed, not when the application is lodged. As the contents of the list can change over time it is advisable to check on DIMIA's website (www.immi.gov.au) before submitting the application.

To be eligible to claim extra points for a job offer in this category, evidence will need to be provided to the Department of Immigration and Multicultural and Indigenous Affairs proving that an offer has been made. The organisation making the job offer must indicate the number of people that it has employed on a full-time basis for the previous two years. DIMIA rigorously checks all applications to ensure that the information is correct.

Australian qualifications

DIMIA recognises that applicants with Australian qualifications have a greater chance of obtaining employment in Australia. Therefore they award extra points for people who have studied for at least 12 months full time and have completed a qualification in Australia.

The qualifications must be at Australian post secondary degree (or higher qualification), diploma, advanced diploma or trade qualification. Five points can be claimed in this category. To receive these points a certified copy of the qualifications and/or notification of results along with a transcript of the academic record must be submitted with the application.

The Department of Immigration and Multicultural and Indigenous Affairs may waive the recent work experience requirements if these Australian qualifications have been completed in the last six months before lodging the migration application. Please note that this six-month period begins from the date of completion of the qualification, and not the date the qualification was conferred.

Spouse skills

If your spouse meets the basic requirements of:

♦ age
♦ English language ability
♦ qualifications
♦ nominated occupation

- recent work experience
- obtained a suitable skills assessment from a relevant assessing authority.

DIMIA is willing to award an extra five points towards the application. Proof that your spouse meets these requirements will be identical to those procedures listed under each of the separate headings above.

If your spouse meets these basic requirements you should carefully consider which person to put forward as the main applicant. Normally it will be best for the main applicant to be the person who receives the highest score. If these details are provided DIMIA will be able to assess both people in the relationship which will help strengthen your application, and give them another option to approve it.

BONUS POINTS

Points may also be claimed for any one of the following:

Capital investment in Australia

If you invest A$100,000 in an approved government investment for a term of at least 12 months, you may qualify for the extra five bonus points. The money should not be invested until the processing officer in charge on your case instructs you to do so. Your intention to do this must be clearly stated in your application.

You should also contact one of the authorities below:

New South Wales Treasury Corporation Registry, GPO Box 7045, Sydney NSW 1115, Australia. Email: nswtcorp@computershare.com.au

Western Australian Treasury Corporation, PO Box 7282, Perth Cloisters Square, WA 6850.
Email: settlement@watc.wa.gov.au

Queensland Treasury Corporation, Level 14, 61 Mary Street, Brisbane QLD 4001, Australia.
Email: smoore@qtc.com.au

Northern Territory Treasury Corporation, GPO Box 2035, Darwin NT 0801, Australia.
Email: territory.bonds@nt.gov.au

South Australian Government Financing Authority, Level 5, 200 Victoria Square, Adelaide SA 5001, Australia.
Email: mckay.mark@saugov.sa.gov.au

Australian work experience

If the applicant has worked legally in Australia in one of the occupations on the Skilled Occupations List for at least six months in the four years before applying they may claim extra bonus points. If this work was done when the applicant was on an Australian bridging visa they will not be eligible to claim points.

Fluency in one of Australia's community languages (other than English)

To be eligible to claim the five bonus points in this category the applicant must have a professional level of language skills (written and oral) in one of the community languages listed below. Evidence of their ability must be provided by either:

◆ qualifications from a university where instruction was in one of the listed languages, or

◆ Accreditation with National Accreditation Authority for Translators Interpreters (NAATI) at a professional level (3).

Afrikaans	German	Polish
Albanian	Greek	Portuguese
Arabic (including	Hindi	Romanian
Lebanese)	Hungarian	Russian
Armenian	Indonesian	Serbian
Bengali	Italian	Sinhalese
Bosnian	Japanese	Slovak
Burmese	Khmer	Slovene
Chinese –	Korean	Spanish
Cantonese	Lao	Swedish
Chinese – Mandarin	Latvian	Tagalog (Filipino)
Croatian	Lithuanian	Tamil
Czech	Macedonian	Thai
Danish	Malaysian	Turkish
Estonian	Maltese	Ukrainian
Fijian	Netherlandic	Urdu
Finnish	(Dutch)	Vietnamese
French	Persian	Yiddish

Relationship

This section is only for applicants applying under the skilled – Australian sponsored category.

You may receive 15 points if you or your spouse have a relative who is:

an Australian citizen or permanent resident, and
is willing to sponsor you.

You or your spouse must be related to the sponsor as either:

◆ a non-dependent child
◆ a parent
◆ a brother or sister
◆ a niece or nephew.

Proof of your or your spouse's relationship to your sponsor must be evidenced by their certificates, marriage certificates and family registers.

An assurance of support must also be provided. You will be advised by DIMIA when your assurer should make an assurance of support application with Centrelink. For more details of what is required your assurer should contact Centrelink on 132 850 or refer to 'assurance of support' details on their website, www.centrelink.gov.au. If overseas call 00 61 3 6222 3455.

A Sponsorship For Migration To Australia, Form 40, must be completed and be submitted with the application.

SKILLED DESIGNATED AREA SPONSORED
To apply within this visa category you are required to meet all of the aforementioned basic requirements, successful skills assessment, age, English language ability and work experience. However, this category is not points tested.

You or your spouse must be related to the sponsor as either a:

- non-dependent child (a natural, adoptive or step-child)
- parent
- brother or sister (including adoptive or step-siblings)
- niece or nephew (including adoptive or step-niece or nephew)
- first cousin or
- grandchild.

You must be able show proof that your relative has been resident in a designated area for at least 12 months prior to you lodging your application.

Designated areas are as follows:

State or Territory	Designated Areas
Victoria	Anywhere
South Australia	Anywhere
Northern Territory	Anywhere
Tasmania	Anywhere
Australian Capital Territory	Anywhere
Queensland	Postcode areas 4019-4028, 4037-4050, 4079-4100, 4114, 4118, 4124-4150, 4158-4168, 4180-4899 (anywhere except Brisbane metropolitan area)
Western Australia	Postcode areas 6042-6044, 6051, 6126, 6200-6799 (anywhere except the Perth metropolitan area)
New South Wales	Postcode areas 2311-2312, 2328-2333, 2336-2490, 2535-2551, 2575-2739, 2787-2898 (anywhere except Sydney, Newcastle and Wollongong)

Proof of your or your spouse's relationship to your sponsor must be evidenced by their certificates, marriage certificates and family registers.

An assurance of support must also be provided. You will be advised by DIMIA when your assurer should make an assurance of support application with Centrelink. For more details of what is required your assurer should contact Centrelink on 132 850 or refer to 'assurance of support' details on their website, www.centrelink.gov.au. If overseas call 00 61 3 6222 3455.

A *Sponsorship For Migration To Australia*, Form 40, must be completed and be submitted with the application.

HEALTH AND CHARACTER CHECKS

Australia has very strict health standards which must be met by any person who is applying to migrate or will be staying in Australia for longer than 12 months.

The health standards are designed to ensure:

♦ Risks to public health and safety in the Australian community are minimised.

♦ Public expenditure on health and community services is contained.

♦ Australian residents have access to health and other community services.

All applicants and dependents who intend to migrate must undertake health screening. This screening will include a physical examination, an X-ray and blood and urine tests.

If the applicant cannot meet the health requirements they will be refused entry unless there are exceptional circumstances.

Tuberculosis

According to the World Health Organisation, tuberculosis is occurring in epidemic levels globally, and presents a serious infectious public health risk.

All people seeking permanent entry who are over 16 years of age must have a radiological exam for tuberculosis. Any applicants under 16 years of age will also need to undergo the exam if they are suspected of having TB or have a history of contact with a person with TB. If the X-ray shows evidence of TB the applicant will be requested to undergo further tests to establish whether or not it is active. If it is active or untreated the person will need to undergo a course of treatment and further tests to confirm that the disease has been adequately treated.

Applicants who have evidence of TB, or have had treatment for TB, may be admitted to Australia but will have to provide a health undertaking which will include follow-up monitoring after their arrival in Australia.

Hepatitis B

While the risk of hepatitis B transmission is low, mandatory screening will apply to:

- pregnant women
- children for adoption
- accompanied minor refugee children.

A positive hepatitis B test will not normally lead to a rejection of the application. The person will normally be required to sign a health undertaking.

HIV/AIDS

All migrants over 15 years of age must undergo HIV/AIDS testing. Applicants under 15 years must also be tested if they have been adopted, undergone blood transfusions, or have any other clinical indications.

The health test procedures

The health checks are normally called for by the DIMIA processing officer after your full migration application has been submitted. If you pass all the other requirements the DIMIA officer will then instruct you to undertake the medicals.

Health checks are normally carried out in the country where the applicant resides, by doctors and radiologists who are approved by the Australian government.

When arranging the medical examinations it is essential that you attend the X-ray examination before seeing the medical doctor, as the X-ray must be available for them to complete the examination.

Character/police checks

To be granted entry to Australia, applicants must be of good character. To determine this, applicants are asked to provide police clearance checks for each country that they have resided in for more than 12 months in the last ten years. It is worth noting that in some countries this process can take anywhere from four weeks to over six months.

In certain circumstances applicants may also be required to provide personal details to enable additional character checks to be undertaken.

As with the medicals this information does not need to be provided when you apply.

APPLYING FOR A VISA

Visa limits
At any stage the Australian government may apply limits (caps) to the number of visas granted each year, or suspend processing applications. If a cap is applied the application will be processed but the visa will not be granted in the year that the visa limits are reached.

Family members
If your other family members are also applying for a visa you will need to decide who to put forward as the primarily applicant. This will generally be the person who has the best chance of meeting the migration requirements. Other family members such as spouses, dependent children or dependent relatives should be included in the same application so you only pay one charge. Children who are born after an application is made, but before a decision has been reached, will automatically be included in the parent application. If this circumstance arises the Australian Mission must be notified of the details of the newborn child. In some circumstances a spouse or dependent child can be added to an application, though they will also need to make certain visa requirements.

Can I lodge more than one application?
If more than one visa is applied for, and approved, the last visa issued will normally be the one that is valid. Thus, any previous visa granted will be null and void. For further advice and clarification the relevant Australian Mission should be contacted.

Withdrawing an application

If you wish to withdraw an application, notice must be lodged in writing with the Australian Mission. Any charges that you have paid to have your case processed will not usually be refunded.

CONTACTING THE AUSTRALIAN MISSION

Change of address

It is the applicant's responsibility to inform the Australian Mission of any change of address that occurs for periods longer than 14 days. The Australian Mission must be informed of the new address and how long you will be staying there. Correspondence will always be sent to the last known address provided and deemed to have been received within 21 days of writing.

Correspondence regarding the application can also be sent to another person or agent, and it will be taken that the applicant has received any letters sent to that person. The Australian Mission must also be informed if you intend to travel to Australia while the application is being processed.

Change of circumstances

The Australian Mission must be informed of any changes of circumstances – for example, a serious illness, change in marital status, the birth of a child – as soon as it is possible and practical. The visa may be cancelled if incorrect information is supplied or you fail to advise the DIMIA that some of the information is no longer correct.

Supplying extra information

Additional information can be provided in writing at any

stage before a decision has been made on the application. In some circumstances they will request or invite you to provide additional information. You will be given a date by which to respond. After that date the application will continue to be considered whether or not you have provided the information requested. DIMIA will not delay the decision-making process if the applicant says they may, or will, give more information later.

Interviews

The Australian Mission may invite you to attend an interview. You will need to agree on the time and date with a DIMIA representative. If you do not attend the interview the application will be processed, and a decision will be made on the basis of the information available. You may be given another opportunity to arrange an interview, but the Australian Mission is not obliged to do this.

HOW YOUR APPLICATION IS PROCESSED

All applications are decided on the basis of two factors: firstly the information that is provided by you, and secondly the law at the time it was submitted. **Applicants should be aware, however, that the government may change the pass mark and pool mark at any time, and this may affect the application.**

It is imperative that applicants thoroughly check through the application and documentation before submitting them for consideration. While it can be a time-consuming and frustrating process gathering together all the information, it must be submitted in the required formats otherwise it will lead to delays in the processing of the case.

8

Family Categories

PROSPECTIVE SPOUSE CATEGORY

Are you engaged to be married to an Australian citizen, Australian permanent resident or eligible New Zealand citizen?

If applying under the prospective spouse category you will need to demonstrate that your relationship is genuine. You will have to show that you intend to marry your fiancé(e) within nine months from the date you are granted a visa and give an undertaking that you intend to live with your partner as their spouse. A further requirement that you and your fiancé(e) are known to each other is included in the criteria.

To satisfy the requirements of this category both you and your fiancé(e) must be aged over 18 years.

For the prospective spouse category, your application must be lodged outside Australia and the applicant at the time of applying must also be outside of Australia.

There are three stages to this application process for this category.

Stage one – prospective marriage temporary visa
The first stage allows you to apply for a temporary visa.

You will need to provide evidence in support of your relationship and complete a medical examination, and provide character/police clearances from any country you have lived in for more than 12 months in the last ten years. If the DIMIA wants to assess the information you have supplied in support of your application they may request you and your fiancé(e) to attend an interview.

If this first stage is approved you will be granted a temporary visa valid for nine months from the date it is issued. Within that time you must travel to Australia, get married and then apply for the spouse temporary category.

Stage two – spouse temporary visa

You must be in Australia when you apply for stage two. You apply for this after your marriage.

You must be in Australia when you apply, complete the application forms, pay the application fee and provide documentary evidence in support of your marriage demonstrating that it is genuine and continuing.

If successful, you will be granted a temporary visa until a decision on your application for a permanent visa is decided. This temporary visa allows for multiple re-entry to Australia.

Stage three – spouse permanent visa

Stage three will commence approximately two years after you lodge your application for spouse category after your initial prospective spouse category application.

At this time DIMIA will require documentary evidence from you and your spouse that your relationship is genuine and continuing, statements from friends or family who know you, your spouse and your circumstances supporting the claim that your relationship is continuing and genuine and an Australian police clearance if you have been living in Australia for more than 12 months. You may be invited to attend an interview by DIMIA. If you meet the requirements your permanent resident's visa will be granted. You must be in Australia at the time the visa is granted.

PROSPECTIVE SPOUSE DOCUMENT CHECKLIST

The following documentation should be forwarded to the Australian High Commission together with the completed Forms 47SP and 40SP.

To be eligible for this category of visa you must be able to show evidence of the following:

◆ You genuinely intend to marry your fiancé(e) within nine months from the date you are granted a visa, and intend to then live with your partner as their spouse. You should provide evidence that you have a celebrant in place to marry you.

◆ You and your fiancé(e) have met and are personally known to each other.

Joint relationship history
◆ A joint signed statement outlining the nature and duration of your relationship:
   1. How, when and where you met.
   2. Details of when you became engaged to marry.

3. How you support each other emotionally and financially (if applicable).
4. Dates when you met each other's families.
5. Dates of joint holidays and travel.
6. Reasons for any periods of separation.
7. Your future plans.

You should also supply any documentary evidence available of the time you have been a couple – photographs, cards and letters/emails and if you have lived together at any time utility bills, bank statements, council tax details, etc.

◆ Four statutory declarations from next of kin, close relatives or friends stating the following:
  1. Their relationship to you both.
  2. How long they have known you as a couple.
  3. They regard you as a genuine couple.
  4. Any other information regarding your relationship that they feel is appropriate.

NB: Statutory declarations must be signed, stamped and witnessed by a solicitor.

Main applicant
1. Certified copy of full length birth certificate for each person included in the application.
2. Certified copy of marriage certificate (if applicable).
3. Certified copies of divorce papers (if applicable).
4. Certified copies of adoption papers (if applicable).

NB: If there are children from a previous marriage or relationship included in the application, a statutory declaration giving permission for the child to leave the UK must be provided by the child/children's other parents.

Identification

1. Certified copy of the identification pages of your passport.
2. Four passport photos for main applicant and any children included in the application (names to be written on reverse of photos).

If you have been self-employed you should provide a letter from your accountant confirming the periods of self-employment together with evidence of tax and national insurance contributions.

Sponsorship (Form 40SP)

Your Australian partner must complete Form 40SP and supply the following documentation:

1. Certified copy of birth certificate.
2. Certified copy of marriage certificate (if applicable).
3. Certified copy of Australian citizenship papers.
4. Certified copy of proof of address in Australia (utility bills) (if applicable).
5. Certified copy of proof of employment (letter from employer or wage slips).
6. Statement confirming that your Australian partner fully supports your application both emotionally and financially.

Police clearances

Each person included in the application who is over the age of 16 years will be required to obtain a police clearance certificate from the relevant Police Authority. Police clearances must also be obtained for any country that you have lived in for more than 12 months in the last ten years. Details can be found on Form 47P.

Medical and radiological examinations
The main applicant will be required to undergo a complete medical and radiological examination by an appointed medical practitioner.

The Australian High Commission is accepting what it calls 'front end loaded' applications. Basically, this means that you provide police clearances and medical examination results at the time of submission of your application.

This does not give any guarantee that your application will be successful, though it does mean that a decision is likely to be made within six weeks of application as opposed to four to six months should you wait until these are requested.

DE FACTO SPOUSE CATEGORY
The de facto category covers relationships where you are living with an Australian citizen, permanent resident or eligible New Zealand citizen. For this category you must satisfy the genuine relationship requirement. This means that you and your partner must have a mutual commitment to a shared life together without marriage. This commitment must be to the exclusion of any other spouse or de facto relationships. You will need to demonstrate that you and your partner are living together, and that you do not live separately or apart on a permanent basis. The relationship must have existed for a minimum period of 12 months before the date of application.

At the time of application you and your partner must be at least 18 years of age.

This category of application is processed in two stages.

Stage one – De facto temporary visa

The first stage will assess your eligibility for a temporary visa under the de facto category. You will need to supply documentary evidence in support of your relationship, undergo a medical examination and submit character/ police clearances for any country in which you have lived for more than 12 months in the last ten years.

If your application is approved at this first stage you will be granted a temporary visa until the time that your application for a permanent visa is decided.

Stage two – De facto permanent visa

Stage two will begin approximately two years after the time that you submitted your temporary visa application. At this time DIMIA will assess your eligibility for a permanent visa.

You will be required to supply documentary evidence in support of your relationship. Your relationship must be genuine and continuing. You will require declarations from friends and family supporting the circumstances of your relationship.

If you have been living in Australia for more than 12 months you will need to supply an Australian police clearance. You and your partner may also be requested to attend an interview by the DIMIA.

DE FACTO CATEGORY DOCUMENT CHECKLIST

The following documentation should be forwarded to the Australian High Commission together with the completed Forms 47SP and 40SP.

Australia's migration regulations stipulate that a de facto relationship is one where the parties have cohabited for at least one year prior to the lodgement of their application.

Joint financial information

1. Certified copies of joint bank account.
2. Wills or life assurance policies made out with the other partner nominated as the principle beneficiary.
3. Certified copies of joint property ownership.
4. Certified copies of joint savings plans or investments.

NB: If a partner has no independent income, evidence must be provided that they are supported by the other partner and have access to their partner's finances.

Joint relationship history

- A joint signed statement outlining the nature and duration of your relationship:
  1. How, when and where you met.
  2. Dates and reasons you commenced cohabitation.
  3. Your domestic arrangements.
  4. How you support each other emotionally and financially.
  5. Dates when you met each other's families.
  6. Dates of joint holidays and travel.
  7. Reasons for any periods of separation.
  8. Your reasons for not marrying.
  9. Your future plans.

- Four statutory declarations from next of kin, close relatives or friends stating the following:
  1. Their relationship to you both.
  2. How long they have known you as a couple.
  3. They regard you as de facto spouses.
  4. Any other information regarding your relationship that they feel is appropriate.

NB: Statutory declarations must be signed, stamped and witnessed by a solicitor.

- Certified copies of the following evidence must also be provided:
  1. Joint mortgage agreement/tenancy agreement.
  2. Joint utility bills – telephone, gas, electricity, cable TV, etc.
  3. Proof of purchase of household items.
  4. Proof of joint travel.
  5. NHS cards.
  6. Official letters showing joint address.
  7. Bank statements.
  8. Driver's licences.
  9. Council tax documentation.

Main applicant
1. Certified copy of full length birth certificate for each person included in the application.
2. Certified copies of divorce papers (if applicable).
3. Certified copies of adoption papers (if applicable).

NB: If there are children from a previous marriage or relationship included in the application, a statutory declaration giving permission for the child to leave the

UK must be provided by the child/children's other parent.

Identification
1. Certified copy of the identification pages of your passport.
2. Four passport photos for main applicant and any children included in the application, and two passport photos of the sponsor (names to be written on reverse of photos).

Education
1. Certified copies of all tertiary qualifications and certificates for the main applicant.

Work experience/employment history
Periods of employment in the last five years must be supported by:

Certified copies of reference, on company letterhead, stating occupation, dates of employment and a list of duties and responsibilities.

If references for each period of employment are not available please provide certified copies of:

1. P60s.
2. Pay advice/wage slips.
3. Job specifications.
4. Letters of appointment.

If you have been self-employed you should provide a letter from your accountant confirming the periods of self-employment together with evidence of tax and national insurance contributions.

Your Australian partner must supply the following information

1. Certified copy of birth certificate.
2. Certified copy of marriage certificate.
3. Certified copy of Australian citizenship papers.
4. Certified copy of proof of address in Australia (utility bills) (if applicable).
5. Certified copy of proof of employment (letter from employer or wage slips).
6. Statement confirming that your partner fully supports your application both emotionally and financially.

Police clearances

Each person included in the application who is over the age of 16 years will be required to obtain a police clearance certificate from the relevant Police Authority. Police clearances must also be obtained for any country that you have lived in for more than 12 months in the last ten years. Details can be found on Form 47P.

Medical and radiological examinations

The main applicant will be required to undergo a complete medical and radiological examination by an appointed medical practitioner.

SPOUSE CATEGORY

The spouse category covers relationships where you are married to an Australian citizen, permanent resident or eligible New Zealand citizen. For this category you must satisfy the genuine relationship requirement. This means that you and your spouse must have a mutual commitment to a shared life. You will need to demonstrate that you and your spouse are in a genuine relationship and that you have not married solely for the purposes of migration. The relationship must have existed for a minimum period of 12 months before the date of application.

At the time of application you and your partner must be 18 years of age or over.

This category of application is processed in two stages.

Stage one – spouse temporary visa

The first stage will assess your eligibility for a temporary visa under the de facto category. You will need to supply documentary evidence in support of your relationship, undergo a medical examination and submit character/ police clearances for any country in which you have lived for more than 12 months in the last ten years.

If your application is approved at this first stage you will be granted a temporary visa until the time that your application for a permanent visa is decided.

Stage two – spouse permanent visa

Stage two will begin approximately two years after the time that you submitted your temporary visa application. At this time DIMIA will assess your eligibility for a permanent visa.

You will be required to supply documentary evidence in support of your relationship. Your relationship must be genuine and continuing.

You will require declarations from friends and family supporting the circumstances of your relationship. If you have been living in Australia for more than 12 months you will need to supply an Australian police clearance. You and your partner may also be requested to attend an interview by the DIMIA.

SPOUSE CATEGORY DOCUMENT CHECKLIST

The following documentation should be forwarded to the Australian High Commission together with the completed Forms 47SP and 40SP. You should provide the following information:

Joint financial information

1. Certified copies of joint bank account.
2. Wills or life assurance policies made out with the other partner nominated as the principle beneficiary.
3. Certified copies of joint property ownership.
4. Certified copies of joint savings plans or investments.

NB: If a partner has no independent income, evidence must be provided that they are supported by the other partner and have access to their partner's finances.

Joint relationship history

◆ A joint signed statement outlining the nature and duration of your relationship:
   1. How, when and where you met.
   2. When and why you decided to marry.
   3. Your domestic arrangements.
   4. How you support each other emotionally and financially.
   5. Reasons for any periods of separation.
   6. Your future plans.

◆ Four statutory declarations from next of kin, close relatives or friends stating the following:

1. Their relationship to you both.
2. How long they have known you as a couple.
3. That your marriage is genuine.
4. Any other information regarding your relationship that they feel is appropriate.

NB: Statutory declarations must be signed, stamped and witnessed by a solicitor.

Main applicant

1. Certified copy of full length birth certificate for each person included in the application.
2. Certified copy of marriage certificate.
3. Certified copies of divorce papers (if applicable).
4. Certified copies of adoption papers (if applicable).

NB: If there are children from a previous marriage or relationship included in the application, a statutory declaration giving permission for the child to leave the UK must be provided by the child/children's other parent.

Identification

1. Certified copy of the identification pages of your passport.
2. Four passport photos for main applicant and any children included in the application, and two passport photos from the sponsor (names to be written on reverse of photos).

Education

Certified copies of all tertiary qualifications and certificates for the main applicant.

Work experience/employment history
Periods of employment in the last five years must be supported by:

Certified copies of reference, on company letterhead, stating occupation, dates of employment and a list of duties and responsibilities.

If references for each period of employment are not available please provide certified copies of:

1. P60s.
2. Pay advice/wage slips.
3. Job specifications.
4. Letters of appointment.

If you have been self-employed you should provide a letter from your accountant confirming the periods of self-employment together with evidence of tax and national insurance contributions.

Your Australian partner must supply the following documentation
1. Certified copy of birth certificate.
2. Certified copy of marriage certificate.
3. Certified copy of Australian citizenship papers.
4. Certified copy of proof of address in Australia (utility bills) (if applicable).
5. Certified copy of proof of employment (letter from employer or wage slips).
6. Statement confirming that your partner fully supports your application both emotionally and financially.

Police clearances

Each person included in the application who is over the age of 16 years will be required to obtain a police clearance certificate from the relevant Police Authority. Police clearances must also be obtained for any country that you have lived in for more than 12 months in the last ten years. Details can be found on Form 47P.

Medical and radiological examinations

The main applicant will be required to undergo a complete medical and radiological examination by an appointed medical practitioner.

The Australian High Commission is accepting what it calls 'front end loaded' applications. Basically, this means that you provide police clearances and medical examination results at the time of submission of your application.

This does not give any guarantee that your application will be successful, though it does mean that a decision is likely to be made within six weeks of application as opposed to four to six months should you wait until these are requested.

INTERDEPENDENT PARTNER CATEGORY

The interdependent category covers same-sex relationships where you are living with an Australian citizen. For this category you must satisfy the genuine relationship requirement. This means that you and your partner must have a mutual commitment to a shared life together. This commitment must be to the exclusion of any spouse or any other interdependent relationships. You will need to demonstrate that you and your partner are living together, and that you do not live separately or apart on a permanent basis. The relationship must have existed for a minimum period of 12 months before the date of application.

Under this category if you have compassionate circumstances due to difficulties living together or cohabitating in the country you have been living in previous to applying then this can be brought to the attention of the DIMIA office.

At the time of application you and your partner must be 18 years of age or over.

This category of application is processed in two stages.

Stage one – Interdependency temporary visa

The first stage will assess your eligibility for a temporary visa under the interdependent category. You will need to supply documentary evidence in support of your relationship, undergo a medical examination and submit character/police clearances for any country in which you have lived for more than 12 months in the last ten years.

If your application is approved at this first stage you will be granted a temporary visa until the time that your application for a permanent visa is decided.

Stage two – Interdependency permanent visa

Stage two will begin approximately two years after the time that you submitted your temporary visa application. At this time they will assess your eligibility for a permanent visa.

You will be required to supply documentary evidence in support of your relationship. Your relationship must be genuine and continuing. You will require declarations from friends and family supporting the circumstances of your relationship. If you have been living in Australia for more than 12 months you will need to supply an Australian police clearance. You and your partner may also be requested to attend an interview by DIMIA. If you and your partner have been in your relationship for five years or more you may not need to fulfil the normal two-year temporary visa period.

INTERDEPENDENT PARTNER CATEGORY DOCUMENT CHECKLIST

The following documentation should be forwarded to the Australian High Commission together with the completed Forms 47SP and 40SP.

Australia's migration regulations stipulate that an inter-dependent relationship is one where the parties have cohabited for at least one year prior to the lodgement of their application.

Joint financial information
1. Certified copies of joint bank account.
2. Wills or life assurance policies made out with the other partner nominated as the principle beneficiary.
3. Certified copies of joint property ownership.
4. Certified copies of joint savings plans or investments.

NB: If a partner has no independent income, evidence must be provided that they are supported by the other partner and have access to their partner's finances.

Joint relationship history

♦ A joint signed statement outlining the nature and duration of your relationship:
  1. How, when and where you met.
  2. Dates and reasons you commenced cohabitation.
  3. Your domestic arrangements.
  4. How you support each other emotionally and financially.
  5. Dates when you met each other's families.
  6. Dates of joint holidays and travel.
  7. Reasons for any periods of separation.
  8. Your future plans.

♦ Four statutory declarations from next of kin, close relatives or friends stating the following:
  1. Their relationship to you both.
  2. How long they have known you as a couple.
  3. They regard you as a genuine couple.
  4. Any other information regarding your relationship that they feel is appropriate.

NB: Statutory declarations must be signed, stamped and witnessed by a solicitor.

♦ Certified copies of the following evidence must also be provided:
  1. Joint mortgage/tenancy agreement.
  2. Joint utility bills telephone, gas, electricity, cable TV, etc.
  3. Proof of purchase of household items.
  4. Proof of joint travel.
  5. NHS cards.
  6. Official letters showing joint address.

7. Bank statements.
8. Council tax documentation.

Main applicant
1. Certified copy of full length birth certificate for each person included in the application.
2. Certified copies of adoption papers (if applicable).

NB: If there are children from a previous marriage or relationship included in the application, a statutory declaration giving permission for the child to leave the UK must be provided by the child/children's other parent.

Identification
1. Certified copy of the identification pages of your passport.
2. Four passport photos for main applicant and any children included in the application, and two passport photos of the sponsor (names to be written on reverse of photos).

Education
Certified copies of all tertiary qualifications and certificates for the main applicant.

Work experience/employment history
Periods of employment in the last five years must be supported by:

Certified copies of reference, on company letterhead, stating occupation, dates of employment and a list of duties and responsibilities.

If references for each period of employment are not available please provide certified copies of:

1. P60s.
2. Pay advice/wage slips.
3. Job specifications.
4. Letters of appointment.

If you have been self-employed you should provide a letter from your accountant confirming the periods of self-employment together with evidence of tax and national insurance contributions.

Your Australian partner must supply the following information

1. Certified copy of birth certificate.
2. Certified copy of Australian citizenship papers.
3. Certified copy of proof of address in Australia (utility bills) (if applicable).
4. Certified copy of proof of employment (letter from employer/wage slips).
6. Statement confirming that your partner fully supports your application both emotionally and financially.

Police clearances

Each person included in the application who is over the age of 16 years will be required to obtain a police clearance certificate from the relevant Police Authority. Police clearances must also be obtained for any country that you have lived in for more than 12 months in the last ten years. Details can be found on Form 47P.

Medical and radiological examinations

The main applicant will be required to undergo a

complete medical and radiological examination by an appointed medical practitioner.

You will be advised by the Australian Mission processing your application when these are required.

PARENT MIGRATION

In March 2003 legislation was passed by the Australian Parliament to allow the number of parent category visas available to be increased tenfold.

There are now four different categories of visa available for parents residing outside of Australia who wish to reside in Australia. There are two classes of visa: the parent visa or the contributory parent visa. The main difference between these two classes of visa is that those applying under the contributory parent visa class are required to make a higher contribution toward their future health costs.

Contributory Parent visa

The two offshore contributory parent visa subclasses are as follows:

- Subclass 143 Contributory Parent (Migrant) visa.
- Subclass 173 Contributory Parent (Temporary) visa.

The threshold requirements for the contributory parent visa categories will be substantially similar to the parent visa categories.

Both categories will have the same first Visa Application Charge (VAC) which is payable at the time of application. This should be confirmed at the time of application.

The key differences would be the level of the second VAC (payable before a visa is granted) and the level and duration of the Assurance of Support bond.

There are significantly more places available under the contributory parent visa categories than for the parent categories. This recognises the fact that contributory parent visa applicants are willing to pay a significantly higher second VAC as a contribution to their ongoing health costs.

There would be two payment options for contributory parent visa applicants:

♦ Permanent visa: pay a **A$25,000** second VAC **per person** (at 1 July 2003, **A$1,080** for dependants under 18); or

♦ Temporary visa: pay a **A$15,000** second VAC **per person** (at 1 July 2003 **A$1,080** for dependants under 18) which would entitle parents to a two-year temporary residence visa including Medicare access and work rights. During that period, parents may apply at any time for a permanent visa at which time the remaining payment of **A$10,000** is required (nil for dependants under 18).

The contributory parent visa category also requires a ten-year, **A$10,000** Assurance of Support bond for main applicants and **A$4,000** for adult secondary applicants (for temporary visa holders, this is payable during processing of the permanent visa).

There are two further categories of visa available, the parent visa and the aged parent visa. Applications made within this visa class will take substantially longer to process than those of the contributory classes.

The basic criteria for these visa categories are based on the same principals as the contributory scheme. The main difference is that you are not required to pay the second VAC.

Aged parent visa

You can apply as an aged parent if you are old enough to be granted an Australian aged pension. You must be the aged parent of a child who is an Australian citizen, Australian permanent resident or eligible New Zealand citizen.

Your child must be a resident in Australia for at least two years before your application is submitted. Your child will have to sponsor or nominate you. Under this category you will also require an assurance of support.

You must pass the balance of family test (see pages 90–91).

Working aged parent

A working aged parent is an applicant who at the time of applying is not at an age where they would be granted an Australian aged pension.

You must be the working aged parent of a child who is an Australian citizen, Australian permanent resident or eligible New Zealand citizen. Your child must have been resident in Australia for at least two years at the time of application.

To be eligible for this category you must pass the balance of family test (see page 94).

You will need to be sponsored by an appropriate person and you will need to provide an assurance of support.

Age requirements

An aged parent is one who is old enough to be granted an Australian aged pension. If you are married only one parent needs to be aged.

Qualifying ages for Australian aged pension	
For men – the qualifying age is 65 years.	
For women – the qualifying age for women depends on their date of birth.	
Date of birth	*Qualifying age*
Before 1 July 1935	60
1 July 1935 – 31 December 1936	60.5
1 January 1937 – 30 June 1938	61
1 July 1938 – 31 December 1939	61.5
1 January 1940 – 30 June 1941	62
1 July 1941 – 31 December 1942	62.5
1 January 1943 – 30 June 1944	63
1 January 1944 – 31 December 1945	63.5
1 January 1946 – 30 June 1947	64
1 July 1947 – 31 December 1948	64.5
1 January 1949 onwards	65

Balance of family test

For parent applications you must pass the balance of family test:

♦ At least half of your children must live in Australia, or

♦ You must have more children living in Australia than in any one other country.

The test is to measure your family links to Australia compared to your family links elsewhere.

Sponsorship/nomination

If you are making your application outside of Australia, you and any dependants included in the application must be sponsored. The sponsor will be required to give a written undertaking to provide support for you during your first two years in Australia, including accommodation and financial assistance if required to meet your family's reasonable living needs.

If you are making your application in Australia, you and any dependants included in the application must be nominated. The nominator does not have to give the same undertaking as a sponsor, but they are still expected to provide assistance to you and your family during the first two years that you are resident in Australia.

A sponsor/nominator must be 18 years or over.

If you are making your application outside Australia generally you must be sponsored by your child (natural, adopted or stepchild) who is a settled Australian citizen, Australian permanent resident or settled eligible New Zealand citizen. The definition of settled for this purpose is being resident in Australia for the previous two years at the time of application.

Assurance of support

All applicants making an application for a parent visa whether aged parent or working aged parent will require an assurance of support.

Your sponsor and assurer do not need to be the same person. The person giving an assurance of support, however, must be over 18 and an adult Australian citizen, Australian permanent resident or eligible New Zealand citizen who is usually resident in Australia and financially able to support the sponsored person and demonstrate their ability to repay certain social security payments should they have been made to people covered by the assurance.

The assurance of support is a commitment to provide financial support to the person applying to migrate so that the applicant will not have to rely on any form of government support. It is also a legal commitment by the person to repay the Commonwealth of Australia any social security payments that may have been made to the person covered by the assurance. The assurance lasts for a stipulated period from the date of arrival in Australia.

An assurer must be able to demonstrate that their taxable income is sustained at a level that would allow them to provide financial support to the applicants whom they assure and also that they would be able to repay any debt incurred by payment of social security payments during the stipulated period.

The assurer will have to undergo an income test. You should confirm the required level of income with Centrelink at the time of application.

PARENT CATEGORIES DOCUMENT CHECKLIST

The following documentation should be supplied together with the completed Forms 47PA/47PT and 40.

Relationship

1. Certified copies of full length birth certificates for each person included in the application.
2. Certified copy of marriage certificate.
3. Certified copies of divorce papers (if applicable).
4. Certified copies of adoption papers (if applicable).

Identification

1. Certified copies of the identification pages of passports
2. Four passport photos for each person included in the application (name to be written on reverse of photos).

Sponsorship (Form 40)

You must provide evidence of your relationship to your child/children in Australia and they will be required to complete the Form 40 and forward it with the following:

1. Certified copy of birth certificate (proving relationship to you).
2. Certified copy of marriage certificate.
3. Certified copy of Australian citizenship papers.
4. Proof of address (utility bills).
5. Proof of employment (letter from employer or wage slips).

Assurance of support

Your sponsor must undertake to assist you with accommodation and financial support if necessary, for a stipulated period immediately following your entry into

Australia. It will also be necessary for your sponsor to lodge an assurance of support with an approved banking institution in Australia. You will be advised when this is required.

Balance of family test
If all your children are living in Australia, your application will receive priority over applications where only an equal number are in Australia and an equal number living overseas. To support the balance of family test you must provide the following evidence from all your children:

1. Full birth certificates proving their relationship to you
2. Adoption certificates (if applicable).
3. Citizenship documents or residency stamps in passports for their usual country of residence.
4. Proof of registration on the electoral roll.
5. Pay and employment advice.

Police clearances
Each person included in the application who is over the age of 16 years will be required to obtain a police clearance certificate from the relevant Police Authority. Police clearances must also be obtained for any country that you have lived in for more than 12 months in the last ten years.

Medical and radiological examinations
Everyone included in the application will be required to undergo a complete medical and radiological examination by an appointed medical practitioner.

You will be advised by the Australian Mission processing your application when these are required.

9

Employer or State/Territory Sponsored Migration

There are five categories for employer or state/territory sponsored migration to Australia:

EMPLOYER NOMINATION SCHEME (ENS)

The Employer Nomination Scheme has been developed to allow Australian employers to recruit permanent, highly-skilled staff from overseas or from people temporarily in Australia, when the employers have been unable to fill a vacancy from within the Australian labour market or through their own training programmes.

The ENS process has two stages:

1. Nomination by an employer.
2. The nominee's application for a visa.

Requirements for an employer

- They have a need for a paid employee, the business is located in Australia and it is operated by the employer.

- The vacancy requires the appointment of a 'highly-skilled person'.

- If applicable, the highly-skilled person is eligible for any mandatory licensing, registration or professional body membership where required.

♦ The position is a full-time, fixed-term appointment of at least three years, which does not exclude the possibility of renewal.

♦ The employer has a satisfactory training record, or for a new business, must make satisfactory provision for future training.

♦ The employer must have demonstrated that the position cannot be filled through the Australian labour market, unless the position is on the Migrant Occupations in Demand List (MODL).

♦ The terms and conditions of employment must be in accordance with the standards for working conditions provided under Australian industrial laws.

Requirements for visa nominee

In general terms, the visa application will be assessed against the following:

♦ The nominee has the skills relevant to the nominated position.

♦ The nominee meets the definition of a 'highly-skilled person'.

♦ The nominee is able to satisfy any mandatory licensing, registration or professional membership requirements.

♦ The employment as outlined in the approved nomination is still available.

♦ The nominee is less than 45 years of age.

♦ The nominee has vocational English language ability.

♦ The nominee and all family members meet mandatory health and character requirements.

REGIONAL SPONSORED MIGRATION SCHEME (RSMS)

This scheme is designed to help employers in regional or low population growth areas of Australia, who have been unable to fill skilled vacancies from the indigenous labour market.

An employer can take part in the scheme if their business is in any area **except** Brisbane, Gold Coast, Newcastle, Sydney, Wollongong, Melbourne and Perth.

Employers considering nominating persons under the RSMS may identify suitable nominees in various ways, including:

♦ through their efforts in testing the local labour market
♦ personal contact and/or experience with the nominee
♦ recommendation from third parties
♦ through the department's skill matching programme.

Skill Matching Database

Skill matching is made possible by the Skill Matching Database. It contains the educational, occupational and personal details of skilled – independent category applicants and skill matching visa applicants.

The Skill Matching Database is updated monthly and distributed to all State and Territory governments and to a network of regional development authorities.

Employers can use the database to identify suitable applicants for nomination under the RSMS or Labour Agreements. Applicants nominated from the database do not need to lodge a further visa application.

The RSMS process
This consists of three stages:

1. Certification of the nomination/vacancy.
2. Nomination by the employer.
3. Nominee's application for a visa.

1. Requirements for certification
In general terms, the employer must be able to demonstrate to a certifying body that:

- the position is a genuine full-time vacancy

- it is available for at least two consecutive years

- it requires qualifications equivalent to at least Australian diploma level (this includes trade certificates)

- the position cannot be filled from the local labour market

- employment and remuneration is in accordance with Australian industrial laws

- there is, or will be, an employment contract or letter of appointment covering the position.

2. Employer nomination assessment
The completed and certified nomination needs to be forwarded to the relevant department business centre, which needs to be satisfied that:

- the nomination has been certified by a regional certifying body;

- all the above conditions were met.

3. Visa nominee requirements

In general terms, the visa application will be assessed against the following:

- the nominee has the relevant qualifications equivalent to at least an Australian diploma

- the nominee is able to satisfy any mandatory licensing, registration or professional membership requirements

- the position is for a fixed term of at least two years (supported by evidence of a contract)

- the nominee is less than 45 years of age

- the nominee has functional English language ability

- the nominee and all family members meet mandatory health and character requirements.

Visa cancellation provisions

Since 1 July 2001, visa cancellation provisions apply where:

- the employee has not commenced employment with the employer within six months of arriving in Australia (or after visa grant if already in Australia); or

- the employee has left the employer within the two year period for reasons within their control.

Cancellation of a visa **will not** occur where a nominating employer terminates an employee's contract within the two year period, provided the employee has made a genuine effort to complete the two years with the approved employer.

If the employee's visa is cancelled, the visas for people who accompanied the employee to Australia, such as family members, will also be cancelled.

LABOUR AGREEMENTS (LA)

Labour Agreements allow Australian employers to recruit (either permanently or temporarily) a specified number of workers from overseas in response to identified or emerging labour market (or skill) shortages in the indigenous labour market. They provide an avenue for either permanent or temporary entry to Australia.

They are also designed to ensure that overseas recruitment supports the longer-term improvement of employment and training opportunities for Australians. Employers or industrial associations are required to make commitments to the employment, education, training and career opportunities of Australians as part of the agreement.

After the agreement has been negotiated, the process consists of two stages:

1. Nomination by the employer.
2. Nominee's application for a visa.

1. Nomination by the employer

In the cases of both temporary and permanent entry, the

employer submits the relevant application form to the business centre managing that labour agreement.

The nomination will be assessed to determine:

◆ the nomination is in accordance with the relevant Labour Agreement

◆ the vacancy falls within the agreed ceiling for the Agreement

◆ the terms and conditions of employment are in accordance with the Agreement

◆ the nominee is under 45 years of age

◆ the nominee has the qualifications and skills (including English language skills) specified in the Labour Agreement.

2. Nominee's application for a visa

In general terms, the visa application will be assessed against the following:

◆ the nominee has the qualifications, skills (including English language skills) and experience specified in the Agreement

◆ the nominee is able to satisfy any mandatory licensing, registration or professional membership requirements under the Labour Agreement

◆ the nominee is less than 45 years of age

◆ the nominee and all family members meet mandatory health and character requirements.

Skill Matching Database

Employers wishing to nominate visa applicants under a Labour Agreement can utilise the Skill Matching Database to identify suitably qualified workers.

The Skill Matching Database contains the educational, occupational and personal details of skilled – independent category applicants and skill matching visa applicants.

Applicants nominated from the database under a Labour Agreement do not need to lodge a further visa application.

The database is updated monthly and distributed to all State and Territory governments and to a network of regional development authorities.

INVEST AUSTRALIA SUPPORT SKILLS (IASS)

This programme is designed to encourage international firms to choose Australia as a location for foreign direct investment. It allows companies that make a significant investment in Australia to bring out essential key expatriate managerial and specialist employees from within the company group (this programme replaced regional headquarters agreements from 1 July 2002).

Agreements are for three years, although individual visas, once granted, may extend beyond the period of the agreement.

IASS agreements are for permanent and/or temporary entry of key managerial and specialist employees. Companies wishing to obtain visas for very small numbers of personnel, or which are seeking staff for existing investments, should access other business immigration programmes.

Applicants must meet **at least one** of the following four criteria for investments of strategic significance to be eligible for the IASS programme:

♦ The project will boost Australian industry innovation through increasing research, development and commercialisation capability, the new application of skills and knowledge technology transfer, and cluster development.

♦ The project will have significant economic benefit to regional Australia taking account of a region's investment needs.

♦ The project's estimated investments are in excess of A$50 million and thus inherently make a significant contribution to economic growth, employment and/or infrastructure.

♦ The company is establishing a regional headquarters or regional operating centre in Australia.

The purpose for the establishment of IASS agreements is different from standard labour agreements in that:

♦ visas granted under IASS agreements are to enable the transfer to Australia of key managerial and specialist employees of the company group

♦ visa applications to which an IASS agreement applies receive priority over applications made under standard Labour Agreements.

IASS agreements provide for either permanent or temporary entry to Australia.

The company submits its proposal to Invest Australia in the Department of Industry, Tourism and Resources (DITR).

Invest Australia will liaise with DIMIA (and other government departments, if necessary) if it decides to proceed with the company's application.

An IASS agreement becomes effective once it has been signed by all parties to the agreement – the manager of Invest Australia, a company representative, and finally, a delegate of the Minister for Immigration and Multicultural and Indigenous Affairs.

After an agreement has been negotiated, the process consists of two stages:

1. Lodgement of the nomination form.
2. Nominee's application for a visa.

SKILLED – STATE/TERRITORY NOMINATED INDEPENDENT (STNI)

This category is for people who are highly skilled and have education, skills and employability which will contribute to the Australian economy, and are willing to settle in states and territories where their skills are in demand.

To apply for this category you must:

- satisfy basic requirements

- nominate a skilled occupation from the Skilled Occupations List

- meet the pool mark for the skilled – independent category

- be nominated by a participating state or territory.

Participating states and territories select nominees to meet a skill shortage in their area.

The State or Territory is **not** the employer. However, as a shortage of skills has been identified, it is anticipated a job may be found quickly.

Successful applicants have a number of obligations, including to:

- remain in the State or Territory for at least two years
- keep authorities informed of changes in address
- take part in surveys as required.

Visas Through Business

The business skills visa class of Australia's migration programme encourages successful business people to settle permanently in Australia and develop new or existing businesses.

Business owners, senior executives and investors can apply for a visa under the business skills category.

On 1 March 2003 a new two-stage process was introduced. Business migrants are granted a business skills (provisional) visa for four years and, after establishing the requisite level of business or maintaining their eligible investment, are eligible to make an application for permanent residence.

An option for permanent residence is still available for high-calibre business migrants sponsored by state/territory governments. This is known as the business talent visa.

The Business Skills Programme is divided into four categories:

- **business owner**: for owners or part-owners of a business

- **senior executive**: for senior executive employees of major businesses

- **investor**: for investors/business people willing to invest in Australia

- **business talent**: for high-calibre business people who have sponsorship from a state/territory government.

In addition, the Business Skills Programme also has two categories for persons who are in Australia on temporary visas, other than the business skills (provisional) visa:

- **established business in Australia (EBA):** for people temporarily in Australia who are owners or part-owners of a business; and

- **regional established business in Australia (REBA):** for people temporarily in Australia who are owners or part-owners of a business in a designated area of Australia.

STATE/TERRITORY GOVERNMENTS

If an Australian State or Territory government business agency wants to attract a particular business or business person to Australia, it can offer to sponsor the applicant.

You may obtain sponsorship in the business owner, senior executive and investor categories.

You must obtain sponsorship in the business talent and regional established business in Australia (REBA) categories.

If the applicant obtains State or Territory government sponsorship, they are entitled to be considered against a lower threshold criteria.

State and Territory governments have their own criteria for deciding whom they will sponsor. The State or Territory government business development agency can provide information on sponsorship, which can be obtained by visiting their website as follows:

Australian Capital Territory – Office of Multicultural Affairs

New South Wales – Business Migrant Information and Referral Service

Northern Territory – Department of Industries and Business

Queensland – Business Migration

South Australia – Business and Skilled Migration

Tasmania – Trade, Marketing and Major Events

Victoria – Business Migration, Industry Victoria

Western Australia – Small Business Development Corporation

BUSINESS OWNER

You must first apply for a business owner (provisional) visa. If you are successful, you will be granted a visa for a period of four years.

Providing you have successfully operated a business in Australia for at least two years and you continue to hold a valid business skills (provisional) visa, you will be eligible to apply for a permanent business owner (residence) visa (permanent residence). You must apply in Australia.

If an applicant has sponsorship from a State or Territory government and applies under the State/Territory sponsored business owner (provisional) or (residence) visa, they are considered against lower threshold criteria.

Provisional visa

To make an application for the business owner (provisional) visa, business owners will need to show that they:

If unsponsored

- have an overall successful business career
- have an ownership interest of at least 10% in a business
- have significant net assets in business
- have significant business and personal assets
- have sufficient net assets to settle in Australia
- have achieved a significant annual turnover in their business
- have a direct and continuous management role in overseas business
- have a commitment to maintain an ownership interest in a business in Australia and direct and continuous involvement in management of that business
- have no history of unacceptable business activities
- are less than 45 years old
- have vocational English.

If sponsored

- are sponsored by a State or Territory government
- have an overall successful business career
- have significant business and personal assets
- have achieved a significant annual turnover in their business or have a continuous employment record at senior level for at least four years

- have sufficient net assets to settle in Australia
- have a direct and continuous management role in overseas business
- have a commitment to maintain an ownership interest in a business in Australia and direct and continuous involvement in management of that business
- have no history of unacceptable business activities
- are less than 55 years old unless exceptional circumstances exist.

Residence visa

To make an application for the business owner (residence) visa, business owners will need to show that they:

If unsponsored
- hold any of the business skills (provisional) visas
- have had an ownership interest in one or more actively operating main business(es) for at least two years
- are involved in strategic management of the business(es)
- employ at least two Australian citizen or permanent resident employees who are not family members
- have substantial business and personal assets
- have substantial net assets in business
- have achieved a significant annual turnover in their business
- have no history of unacceptable business activities
- have been in Australia as the holder of a qualifying visa for at least one year in the last two years.

If sponsored
- are sponsored by a State or Territory government
- hold any of the business skills (provisional) visas or a temporary business (long stay) independent executive visa

- have had an ownership interest in one or more actively operating main business(es) for at least two years
- are involved in strategic management of the business
- have substantial net assets in the business or have substantial net business and personal assets or employ at least one Australian citizen or permanent resident employee who is not a family member (you must meet two out of these three points unless you are able to provide a waiver from the sponsoring State/Territory)
- have achieved a significant annual turnover in their business
- have no history of unacceptable business activities
- have been in Australia as the holder of a qualifying visa for at least one year in the last two years.

SENIOR EXECUTIVE

To make an application for the senior executive (provisional) visa, senior executives will need to show that they:

If unsponsored
- have an overall successful business career
- are employed in one of the top three levels of management of a major business
- have significant business and personal assets
- have sufficient net assets to settle in Australia
- have a commitment to maintain an ownership interest in a business in Australia and direct and continuous involvement in management of that business
- have no history of unacceptable business activities
- are less than 45 years old
- have vocational English.

If sponsored
- are sponsored by a State or Territory government

- have an overall successful business career
- are employed in one of the top three levels of management of a major business
- have significant business and personal assets
- have sufficient net assets to settle in Australia
- have a commitment to maintain an ownership interest in a business in Australia and direct and continuous involvement in management of that business
- are less than 55 years old unless exceptional circumstances exist.

INVESTOR

This section contains information on who can apply for migration to Australia under the investor category (unsponsored or sponsored).

Provisional visa

To make an application for the investor (provisional) visa, investors will need to show that they:

If unsponsored

- have a successful record of business or investment management
- are willing to make a significant investment in a government approved designated investment for four years
- have significant business and personal assets
- have sufficient net assets to settle in Australia
- have no history of unacceptable business activities
- are less than 45 years old
- have vocational English.

If sponsored

- are sponsored by a State or Territory government and

intend to live in that state or territory for a minimum of two years
- have a successful record of business or investment management
- are willing to make a significant investment in a government approved designated investment for four years
- have significant business and personal assets
- have sufficient net assets to settle in Australia
- have no history of unacceptable business activities
- are less than 55 years old, unless exceptional circumstances exist.

Residence visa

To make an application for the investor (residence) visa, investors will need to show that they:

If unsponsored
- hold an investor (provisional) visa
- have maintained their designated investments for the minimum four years
- have been in Australia as the holder of a qualifying visa for at least two years in the last four years.

If sponsored
- are sponsored by a State or Territory government
- hold a State/Territory sponsored investor (provisional) visa
- have maintained their designated investments for the minimum four years
- have been resident in the sponsoring State or Territory as the holder of a qualifying visa for at least two years in the last four years.

BUSINESS TALENT

High-calibre business persons may apply for direct permanent residence in the first instance. If you are successful you will be granted a permanent visa.

To make an application for the business talent visa, business people will need to show that they:

- are sponsored by a State or Territory government
- have an overall successful business career
- have significant net assets in business
- have significant business and personal assets
- have achieved a significant annual turnover in their business
- have a commitment to maintain an ownership interest in a business in Australia and direct and continuous involvement in management of that business
- have no history of unacceptable business activities
- are less than 55 years old unless exceptional circumstances exist.

ESTABLISHED BUSINESS IN AUSTRALIA

Business people who establish a business in Australia can only apply to migrate under the established business in Australia category while they are in Australia with a temporary visa other than a bridging visa or a criminal justice visa.

You will need to show that you have had at least 10% ownership in an Australian business, for at least 18 months prior to lodging your application.

To be eligible to apply to migrate to Australia under the

Established Business in Australia category you will need to show that:

- you are the holder of a temporary substantive visa – that is, a visitor, student or temporary resident visa other than a special purpose, border, diplomatic, domestic worker or transit visa

- you have been in Australia for a minimum of nine months cumulatively in the 12 months before the date of application

- you have held an ownership interest of at least 10% in one or more main businesses in Australia for at least 18 months immediately before applying

- your (or your and your spouse's) total net assets in Australia for the 12 months prior to application were greater than A$250,000

- your (or your and your spouse's) net assets in business in Australia for the 12 months prior to application were greater than A$100,000

- you have been actively involved in, and directly responsible for, the day-to-day management and overall performance of your main business(es)

- you have an overall successful business career

- you have not been involved in business or investment activities considered unacceptable in Australia

- you score at least **105 points** in the established business in Australia points test. The points test categories are age, language ability, business attributes and net assets.

REGIONAL ESTABLISHED BUSINESS IN AUSTRALIA (REBA)

Under the regional established business in Australia category, you need to:

◆ be in Australia and hold a business (long stay) 457 visa

◆ have had an ownership interest in a main business in a designated area of Australia for at least two years immediately before you apply (and continue to have an interest of that kind)

◆ be registered with a State/Territory government authority which will provide sponsorship when the application is decided.

Main business

To qualify:

◆ you (or you and your spouse) must own at least 10% of its value

◆ you must be actively involved in its day-to-day management

◆ it must be active, providing goods and/or services to the public and not set up primarily for speculative or passive investment purposes.

You may have up to two main businesses.

Designated areas

◆ These are all of Victoria, South Australia, Tasmania, Australian Capital Territory and Northern Territory

- New South Wales – entire state except Sydney, Newcastle and Wollongong

- Queensland – entire state except Brisbane, Sunshine Coast and Gold Coast

- Western Australia – entire state except Perth metropolitan region.

Criteria	REBA visa subclass 846
Total net assets in Australia	A$200,000
Net assets in business in Australia	A$75,000
Turnover	$200,000 or exports of at least A$100,000
Points test	105
Persons employed	Must have had at least two full-time employees or part-time pro-rata equivalent throughout a **two-year** period to score points.
Period of residence	Must have been in Australia as a temporary resident for at least **12 months** out of the last 24 months immediately before applying.
Ownership interest	Must have held an ownership interest of at least 10% in one or more established main businesses **in a designated area** in Australia for at least **two years** immediately before applying, and continue to have an interest of that kind.

OBLIGATIONS AFTER ARRIVAL AND POINTS SELF-TESTS

Please note that any points described in this outline are relevant on the date of publication. For up-to-date information on the points contact your nearest Australian Consulate or Mission.

Business owner

You must notify an Australian State or Territory Government business development agency of your intention to engage in business in Australia and score at least 105 points in the business owners points test.

All applicants for a business skills visa have to meet specific obligations after their arrival in Australia and must sign a declaration stating that they will adhere to these standards. In signing this form they acknowledge that if they do not make genuine efforts to participate in business within three years of the visa being granted (whether the visa was issued in or out of Australia) then DIMIA have the right to cancel that visa and the visas of their family.

The obligations for a business owner are that they will:

- obtain a substantial ownership interest in an eligible business in Australia – this business may be new or existing as long as it does one or more of the following:
  - creates international market links, maintains or increases employment in Australia
  - exports Australian made goods or services or produces goods that would otherwise be imported
  - improves or introduces new technology to Australia and improves commercial activity and competitiveness within sectors of the Australian economy.

- keep DIMIA informed of their current address for three years

♦ participate in DIMIA'S monitoring surveys.

Applications can be made for this category from either outside or inside Australia.

Business owner self-test

Age at the time of application	Points
20–29	20
30–44	30
45–49	25
50–54	10
Under 20	0
Over 55	0

Language ability at decision:

Better than functional English	30
Functional English	20
Bilingual in non-English languages	10
Limited English	10
No English	0

Turnover

If your main business(es) had an annual turnover, in the last of the 4 fiscal years before your application, of:

A$5,000,000 +	60
A$3,000,000 +	55
A$1,500,000 +	50
A$750,000 +	40
A$500,000 +	35
Less than A$500,000	0

Labour costs

If your main business(es) had annual costs, in two of the last four fiscal years before your application, of:

Minimum A$500,000	10
Minimum A$250,000	5
Less than A$250,000	0

Total assets

If your main business(es) had total assets, in two of the last four fiscal years before your application, of:

Minimum A$1,500,000	10
Minimum A$750,000	5
Less than A$750,000	0

Net assets at decision

If your (or your spouse's) net assets, available for transfer to Australia within two years are:

Minimum A$2,500,000	15
Minimum A$1,500,000	10
Minimum A$500,000	5
Less than A$500,000	0

Sponsorship

If you are sponsored by an authorised Australian State/Territory development agency   15

Senior executive category

You must show that you intend to engage in business as a substantial owner in an Australian company and have notified an Australian State/Territory government business agency (note that an approved form 927 from an above named agency must be submitted with your application and that you must also complete form 1137 a business skills profile). You must score at least 105 points on the senior executive category points test.

All applicants for a business skills visa have to meet specific obligations after their arrival in Australia and must sign a declaration stating that they will adhere to these standards. In signing this form they acknowledge that if they do not make genuine efforts to participate in business within three years of the visa being granted (whether the visa was issued in or out of Australia) then DIMIA have the right to cancel that visa and the visas of their family.

The obligations for a senior executive are that they will:

◆ obtain a substantial ownership interest in an eligible business in Australia – this business maybe new or existing as long as it does one or more of the following:
  – creates international market links
  – maintains or increases employment in Australia
  – exports Australian made goods or services or produces goods that would otherwise be imported
  – improves or introduces new technology to Australia and improves commercial activity and competitiveness within sectors of the Australian economy.

◆ keep DIMIA informed of their current address for three years

◆ participate in DIMIA's monitoring surveys.

Applications can be made for this category from either outside or inside Australia.

Senior executive self-test

Age at the time of application	Points
20–29	20
30–44	30
45–49	25
50–54	10
Under 20	0
Over 55	0

Language ability at decision

Better than functional English	30
Functional English	20
Bilingual in non-English languages	10
Limited English	10
No English	0

Business attributes

If the major business which has employed you has had, in two of the last four fiscal years before your application, an annual turnover of:

If unsponsored A$50,000,000 +	65
If sponsored A$10,000,000 +	65

Net Assets

If your (or your spouse's) net assets, available for transfer to Australia within two years, are:

Minimum A$2,500,000	15
Minimum A$1,500,000	10
Minimum A$500,000	5
Less than A$500,000	0

Established business in Australia category

You must score 105 points in the established business in Australia category points test.

All applicants for a business skills visa have to meet specific obligations after their arrival in Australia and must sign a declaration stating that they will adhere to these standards.

The obligations of owners of an established business in Australia are that they will:

♦ intend to maintain their ownership interest in an eligible business in Australia

♦ keep DIMIA informed of their current address for three years

♦ participate in DIMIA's monitoring surveys.

Applications can only be made for this category from inside Australia.

Established business in Australia self-test

Age at the time of application	Points
20–29	20
30–44	30
45–49	25
50–54	10
Under 20	0
Over 55	0

Language ability at decision

Better than functional English	30
Functional English	20
Bilingual in non-English languages	10
Limited English	10
No English	0

Business attributes

If for one year prior to application your main   60
business(es): employed three full time (or
equivalent) Australian permanent residents (who
are non family members), and had a minimum
annual turnover of A$200,000 or had exports of
minimum A$100,000 a year.

Net assets

If your (or your spouse's) net assets, available
for transfer to Australia within two years are:

Minimum A$2,500,000	15
Minimum A$1,500,000	10
Minimum A$500,000	5
Less than A$500,000	0

Regional established business in Australia category

You must score a minimum of 105 points in the
established regional business in Australia points test and
complete a business skills profile form 1138.

All applicants for a business skills visa have to meet
specific obligations after their arrival in Australia and
must sign a declaration stating that they will adhere to
these standards.

The obligations of owners of a regional established
business in Australia are that they will:

◆ intend to maintain their ownership interest in an
eligible business in Australia

◆ keep DIMIA informed of their current address for three years

◆ participate in DIMIA's monitoring surveys.

Applications can only be made for this category from inside Australia.

Regional established business self-test

Age at the time of application	Points
20–29	20
30–44	30
45–49	25
50–54	10
Under 20	0
Over 55	0

Language ability at decision

Better than functional English	30
Functional English	20
Bilingual in non-English languages	10
Limited English	10
No English	0

Business attributes

If for the two years prior to application
your main business(es) employed:
three full time (or equivalent) Australian
permanent residents, citizens or eligible
New Zealand citizens (who are not
family members)   60
at least two full time (or equivalent)
Australian permanent residents, citizens or
eligible New Zealand citizens (who are not
family members)   40

Net assets
If your (or your spouse's) net assets, available
for transfer to Australia within two years are

Minimum A$2,500,000	15
Minimum A$1,500,000	10
Minimum A$500,000	5
Less than A$500,000	0

Sponsorship
If you are sponsored by a State or Territory
government business agency   15

Investor category
You must complete a business skills profile form 1139 and
score a minimum of 105 points in the investor points test.

All applicants for a business skills visa have to meet
specific obligations after their arrival in Australia and
must sign a declaration stating that they will adhere to
these standards.

The obligations owners of a regional established business
in Australia are that they will:

♦ intend to maintain their investment or business
  activities in Australia after the three-year term of
  their investment expires

♦ keep DIMIA informed of their current address for
  three years

♦ participate in DIMIA's monitoring surveys

♦ have their visa cancelled if they withdraw the
  designated investment before the three-year period is
  completed.

Applications can be made for this category from either outside or inside Australia.

Investor self-test

Age at the time of application	Points
20–29	20
30–44	30
45–49	25
50–54	10
Under 20	0
Over 55	0

Language ability at decision

Better than functional English	30
Functional English	20
Bilingual in non-English languages	10
Limited English	10
No English	0

Business (investment) attributes

If you have deposited, for a minimum three year term, a designated investment of:

Minimum A$2,000,000	80
Minimum A$1,500,000	70
Minimum A$1,000,000	65
Minimum A$750,000	60

COST AND CHARGES

As application charges can change without notice, it is best to check with any Australian mission or DIMIA office for the latest figures. All fees and charges are normally stated in Australian dollars, so if you are applying within Australia by mail the preferred method of payment is money order, bank cheque or credit card. If you are applying within Australia in person the preferred method of payment is by debit or credit card. If you are applying outside of Australia the Mission can inform you of what payment method to use and what the cost would be in your relevant currency.

Payment is normally made in instalments. The first application charge covers you and your family – it is important to note that this charge is non-refundable regardless of the outcome of your visa.

The second instalment is for those who are assessed as **not** having *functional English*.

There is a cost for you and additional costs for any other candidates on your application. This payment covers the cost of English tuition in Australia to achieve a *functional English* level. Please note that this second instalment must be paid in full before your visa will be granted.

As part of your application you may also be required to pay for a medical examination for each of your family members included in the assessment. Additional costs will arise within the application process so be aware that you will need to pay for these. They may include character clearances from authorities and certified translations of some documents.

DEPENDANTS

Your application may cover your family, including you and your spouse and any dependants. Your spouse is defined as the person that you live with as husband and wife either legally married or in common law as a de facto relationship. Dependent children are defined as under the age of 18 who are not married or in a de facto relationship or engaged to be married. They may be natural, adopted or a step-child. Children aged 18 or over should apply separately unless you can prove that they are substantially reliant on you for financial support and have been for some time for their basic needs of food, shelter and clothing.

11

Child and Other Family Migration

Child migration is migration to Australia as the dependent child, orphan relative or adopted child of an Australian citizen, Australian permanent resident or eligible New Zealand citizen.

Within all of the following categories the child must be sponsored by an Australian citizen, Australian permanent resident or eligible New Zealand citizen.

The child category is for the natural, adopted or step-child of a sponsor. Where a child was adopted after the sponsor became a permanent resident, they should apply under the adopted child category.

Please note that a child can only be granted a permanent child visa based on a step-relationship if the child's natural or adopted parent is no longer the spouse of the step-parent and that step-parent has been granted legal responsibility for the child by a court.

ORPHAN RELATIVE CATEGORY
The orphan relative category is for a child under 18 years of age who has no parent to care for them.

ADOPTION CATEGORY

This category is for a child under 18 years of age who has been adopted or is in the process of being adopted by their sponsor.

The adoption must be supported by a state or territory welfare authority, unless the adoptive parent has been resident for a minimum period of 12 months at the time the migration application is lodged.

The adoptive parent must be able to demonstrate that their residence overseas was not contrived for the purpose of bypassing the requirements concerning entry of the adopted child.

DEPENDENT CHILD (TEMPORARY) CATEGORY

This category is for the natural, adopted or step-child of the holder of a provisional partner visa.

The dependent child visa is a provisional visa which allows the dependent child of the holder of a provisional partner visa to travel to or remain in Australia for the same period as their parent.

Once this visa has been granted the holder can apply to be included in their parent's permanent partner visa application.

OTHER FAMILY MIGRATION

Other family migration is migration to Australia on the basis of being an aged dependant relative, remaining relative or the carer of an Australian citizen, Australian permanent resident or eligible New Zealand citizen.

Within each of the other family migration categories you must be sponsored by an Australian citizen, Australian permanent resident or eligible New Zealand citizen.

AGED DEPENDENT RELATIVE

Those who can apply under this category are people who are single, widowed or divorced aged person who are dependant on a relative who lives in Australia (see below for definition of relative).

REMAINING RELATIVE

Those who can apply under this category are the brother, sister or child (or step-relative the same) of a person in Australia, who, if they did not migrate to Australia would otherwise be left on their own overseas.

CARER

Those who can apply under the carer category are people who are willing and able to give substantial and continual assistance to an Australian relative (or a member of their family) who has a medical condition causing physical, intellectual or sensory impairment of their ability to attend to the practical aspects of daily life.

Definition of relative

Relatives include child, parent, sibling, grandparent, grandchild, uncle, aunt, niece or nephew (or step-relative the same).

12

Useful Information

ARRIVING

Nearly all visitors to Australia arrive by air. The main international airports are:

Adelaide	Darwin	Perth
Brisbane	Hobart	Sydney
Cairns	Melbourne	

On board your aircraft you will be handed an arrival card called an 'Incoming Passenger Card' – every person entering the country must fill out one of these.

At each airport there are services to help you with information, car rental, hotel bookings, internal flights, taxis and bus services into the city.

Passport

All visitors are required to have a valid passport, onward or return tickets and enough money to support them during their entire visit.

Visas

All visitors need a visa to visit Australia. The one exception to this rule is anyone holding a New Zealand passport – they are allowed to enter with just a passport.

Visitor visas are free and are valid for visits of up to three months. If you are travelling for longer then you will require a visa that is valid for up to a maximum period of six months and these are currently valued at A$30. Tourist visas are issued by the Australian Consulate Office within your country and must be obtained before you leave home.

Inoculations
Inoculations are generally not required unless during the two weeks before your arrival you have been in a country infected with typhoid, yellow fever, smallpox or cholera.

Customs regulations
At the time you receive your arrival card you will also be given a 'Travellers Statement'. This must be read, filled out and adhered to carefully. Each traveller may bring in the following articles free of tax and duty, providing that they are not intended for commercial purposes and that they accompany you through Customs:

- 250gms of tobacco products (this is equivalent to 250 cigarettes) per person over 18 years of age

- 1125mls of alcohol liquor – beer, wine or spirits – per person over 18 years of age

- all personal clothes and footwear – excluding fur apparel

- articles for personal grooming and hygiene – excluding perfume concentrate and jewellery

- all visitors' goods provided you intend to take them out of the country when you leave

- articles taken out of Australia on departure but not including articles purchased duty and or sales tax free in Australia – any duty/tax free goods are counted against your duty free allowance

- other articles (not tobacco or alcohol) obtained overseas or duty and sales tax free in Australia up to and not exceeding a total purchase price of A$400 per person 18 years or older, or A$200 per person under 18 years. Please note this does include goods intended as gifts or received as gifts and jewellery, whether personal, a gift or carried on behalf of others.

Members of the same family travelling together can complete one statement that covers a husband, wife and children under 18 years of age. They may also combine their individual duty free allowances.

Travellers may bring in more than their allocated amount including tobacco and alcohol as long as they declare the excess and pay the duty and/or tax owing. Unaccompanied baggage whether posted or shipped does not attract any duty free concessions unless you have owned and have used the items for 12 months or more.

Australia has strict laws prohibiting and restricting the entry of drugs, steroids, firearms and other weapons. If you are carrying any goods that you think may fall into any of these categories or are subject to quarantine, then you must declare this to Customs upon your arrival.

There are no restrictions on the amount of currency that can be taken into or out of Australia. However, amounts of A$5,000 or more must be reported on arrival or departure.

Please note that these details are correct at the time of printing. For up-to-date information or clarification on any of these issues, please contact the Australian Mission or local travel agent within your country.

Agricultural restrictions
Like most South Pacific countries Australia is very fortunate in that it lacks many plant and animal diseases and it is also relatively pest free. With the aim of keeping Australia in this situation, the Quarantine Department has various strict regulations on the importation of foods, animals and plants into Australia. It is safest to assume that anything of this nature is prohibited.

Departure tax
All travellers must pay a departure tax. This can be organised through your travel agent and included into your airline ticket cost or paid at any post office within Australia or at the airport before you leave. Currently the departure tax stands at A$25.

MONEY MATTERS
Since 1966 Australia has had a decimal currency – dollars and cents. Coins are available in 5, 10, 20 and 50 cent and A$1and A$2 pieces, and notes come in A$5, A$10, A$20, A$50 and A$100 denominations. As Australia leads the world in banknote printing, notes are now printed on a special plastic, which makes forging difficult.

All well known traveller's cheques and credit cards are accepted, including American Express, Mastercard, Visa and Diner's Club. Most foreign currencies can be changed at the airport, city banks, international class hotels and Bureaux de Change. Be aware that these services are only supplied in major tourist destinations so it best to make sure you have enough money before embarking on an outing.

TRANSPORT

Car rental

Car rental operators within Australia include Budget, Hertz and Avis, all of which have very similar rates. Other smaller operators may offer cheaper cars, but you should look closely at the insurance and excess prices as they could make the end price a lot higher. Most companies will only rent to drivers 25 years or older and you will need to provide your home country's licence or an international licence – these are valid within Australia for a period of up to one year.

Driving

Road rules to remember include:

♦ Australians drive on the left.

♦ Always give way to your right.

♦ Keep your seat belt fastened at all times – this applies to every passenger in the car.

♦ General speed limits include 60kph in built-up areas and 100kph–110kph in the country depending on which state you are in.

♦ There is random breath testing for alcohol throughout the country. The safest advice is not to drink and drive at all, but you will get charged if your blood-alcohol level exceeds 0.05 per cent.

Petrol costs around 70 cents a litre in the cities and more once you get out into the country. Diesel and unleaded fuel are readily available and regular leaded fuel is being phased out slowly. Most service stations are self-service with automatic pumps. A wide range of credit cards are accepted at large service stations, but beware that the smaller stations may only accept Visa and Mastercard. Also remember that distances in Australia are vast and that inland country towns are often very far apart. It is wise to work out the distances you are travelling and where you are going to be able to stop and fill up – this will ensure that you do not run out of petrol in a very isolated part of the country.

Air transport

Both of Australia's international airlines offer internal flights – as Australia is such a vast and empty country the only practical way to tackle long distances and extensive travel is by air. Qantas and Ansett Australia Airlines offer domestic networks alongside a few other smaller feeder airlines. There is little real difference in service between the main competition, but there is a range of discount fares available for international travellers – provided you book these before you leave your home country. Every town and city of any size has an airfield, as do many individual properties in the country, and most business travel is also done by air.

Trains

A vast network of railways operates from one end of the nation to the other – although it is not as comprehensive as some other countries' railway systems. Modern air conditioned trains operate on the outback and coastal routes. The main lines follow the east and south coasts, linking the cities of Cairns, Brisbane, Sydney, Melbourne and Adelaide. Lines from Adelaide connect into the line between Sydney and Perth. If you plan to do a lot of travel by train you should buy an 'Austrailpass', which gives you unlimited travel in first or economy class on interstate or metropolitan trains. This pass can only be purchased overseas by the holder of a foreign passport.

Ferries
The only regular interstate ferry services that operate are 'The Spirit of Tasmania' which links between Melbourne and Devonport and the 'Seacat' which links Port Welshpool in Victoria and George Town in Tasmania.

Sydney has its own urban ferries and cruises that operate across the harbour, and Perth also has a ferry link across the Swan River.

Long distance coaches
The standard of all coaches on nationwide services is high. Most have air conditioning, reclining seats and toilets. Again if you plan to do extensive travel by coach then there are discount plans available and do check what services are offered on board.

Urban transport
Urban transport networks range from good to adequate. Sydney, Mebourne, Brisbane, Adelaide and Perth all offer bus and train services. Hobart, Canberra and Darwin only offer a bus service.

Taxis
Except for in some country towns all Australian taxis operate on a meter system. Fares are displayed on the

meter and all drivers must display a photo and identification card. You can stop and hire a taxi whenever you see one or at an extra charge make a phone booking. Smoking is not permitted in many public vehicles so it is advisable to ask your driver first.

UTILITIES

Electricity
Supply in Australia is 220–240 volts, and this is very dependable throughout the entire country. Outlets for 110 volt shavers are found in many hotels and motels, but for other appliances like hairdryers you will need a converter and a special flat three-pinned adapter. The best place to buy adapters is at the airport in your home country as you are leaving.

Water
All towns and cities within Australia have clean and healthy public water supplies. Tap water is safe to drink. Bottled mineral water is also available everywhere.

TIME AND HOLIDAYS

Time
Australia has three time zones for most of the year:

- Eastern Standard Time – Queensland, Canberra, New South Wales, Victoria and Tasmania – ten hours ahead of Greenwich Mean Time.

- Central Australian Time – South Australia and Northern Territory – are nine-and-a-half-hours ahead.

- Western Standard Time – Western Australia – eight hours ahead.

During the summer months daylight savings complicates this pattern:

- Western Australia and Queensland do not have daylight saving.
- The other states start and finish it at different times.

Public holidays

The National holidays are:

- New Year's Day (1 January)
- Australia Day (26 January)
- Good Friday
- Easter Saturday
- Easter Monday
- Anzac Day (25 April)
- Queen's Birthday (second Monday in June, except for Western Australia where it is the last weekend in September)
- Christmas Day (25 December)
- Boxing Day (26 December)
- Each state also has an additional public holiday of its own.

All banks, post offices, private offices, government and shops are closed on the above mentioned holidays.

WEATHER

Australia is situated in the southern hemisphere, which means that the seasons are at the opposite times to Europe or North America.

- December to February – summer
- March to May – autumn
- June to August – winter
- September to November – spring

As Australia covers such a vast area, each territory has it own climates and each slightly differs in the season that you should visit:

Northern Territory and Queensland

November to March is when the wet, or as it is more commonly known by the locals 'green season', is in force. As these two territories have very tropical climates this is the ideal period in which to visit these unique areas.

Tasmania

Tasmania is far enough south so that summer is the best season to enjoy this beautiful part of Australia.

Mainland

Spring and autumn are the ideal travelling periods within these territories.

Western Australia

Spring is when Western Australia comes to life – the flowers are out and the temperatures are just right.

Sydney

Summers can get very hot and humid in Sydney but the beaches are plentiful.

Being prepared

Winter in Australia can be similar to Europe depending on where you live. In Melbourne the seasons can vary within a day, requiring a jacket, scarf and umbrella but when the rain passes be prepared to take it all off. Up the coast in the north, however, the temperature never drops off entirely – in summer you wear shorts and a tee shirt and in winter, light trousers and a sweatshirt. Most of Australia never sees snow but there is one region where you can go skiing.

WHERE TO LIVE

If you are immigrating permanently one of your main questions will be 'Where am I going to live?'. Australia varies in both climate and region, which means that you will find the perfect area and community to suit your lifestyle. Every city and large town has a large choice of suitable housing options and community services to cater to all your needs, which will guarantee you and your family a very comfortable environment in which to live.

Cities like Melbourne, Sydney, Brisbane, Perth and Adelaide, which all have over one million people living within the cities parameters, present a variety of housing which can satisfy even the most demanding tastes. However, given the high standard of housing, these large cities compare extremely well to other main cities in the world, in that the housing prices are relatively low. It is quite normal, for example, for a quite modest house in Australia to have a swimming pool and a reasonable section of land out the back, while the surrounding community area will be dotted with playing fields and tennis courts for everyone to have use of.

Australian houses are typically a mixture of European and American styles with an Australian twist. As the climate varies throughout the country the building materials for houses also vary. In Queensland the climate is tropical and the houses tend to be quite open plan and built from timber. In Melbourne the weather incorporates the four seasons so there is more brick and a lot more fireplaces.

There is a strong sense of space and privacy, as the traditional goal of a 'home on a quarter acre block of land' has strongly influenced the format of the suburbs in most of Australia's towns and cities. This makes the communities within the cities very comfortable places to reside in.

Until recently the inner city areas throughout Australia were used for commercial business reasons only. It has only become popular in the last 20 years for people to live this close in as more and more people have discovered the excitement and convenience of inner city living. You therefore will not see the high rise concentration of Asia, America and Europe.

As in other large cosmopolitan cities, housing costs more in the centre of the city than in the smaller towns. The same house found in Melbourne or Sydney would cost more than double what it would in another city like Hobart. The advantage of living in a large city like Sydney is the choice that is available to you, from waterside mansions and suburban homes to convenient and comfortable inner city apartments.

House prices vary so much across the country that it is difficult to give a simple picture of what a house would cost. The best way to evaluate the housing market would be to contact your local Australian Mission for the latest information, and do remember that there are great differences across the country. This means that you will be able to find the right kind of house for you and your family, in the right area or the kind of lifestyle you wish to achieve, at the right price.

Buying or renting

Home ownership is incredibly popular in Australia with over 70% of the population in some cities living in property owned by them. If you are looking to buy then this is fully encouraged by banks, credit unions, building societies and other financial institutions, as they offer up to 90% of the value of the property, depending on the borrower's financial status.

Most houses and units in Australia are sold through established real estate agents. These businesses have the expertise to complete the required transactions with relative ease and they are also governed by regulations which means that everything is done in accordance with the law. If you are looking to rent, real estate agents have a section within their offices that deals with houses, units and apartments to rent. Again you will be able to locate something that will be of interest to you, given the extensive range that is available. Other places to research houses to buy and rent would be the local and national newspapers, community notice boards and the internet.

The latest way to buy or build your home in Australia is by visiting a home village display. Interestingly Sydney boasts the world's largest home and display villages. Some villages have up to 100 designs on show, so finding the right home for you could not be made any easier. The houses on display at the exhibition villages are the products of Australia's biggest builders and leading specialist builders, and the villages give these businesses the ability to showcase their very latest designs and best-selling homes.

The advantage of this type of village is that you can choose the design you like, view the home as it will be once it has been completed and discuss what the best type of building material requirements are for you – given the region you have chosen to live in. This 'one stop' shop enables you to choose a block of land from dozens of locations, and arrange finance on the spot. To visit the two major display villages in Sydney you can contact the manager of both HomeWorld and Housing World at: PO Box 569, Epping NSW 2121. Tel: + 612 869 8900. Fax: + 612 868 2056.

If you are building outside of Sydney, then a visit to these exhibition homes is a must, as there are also many builders that construct homes all over New South Wales. For up-to-date information on display villages both in and outside of Sydney, contact your local Australian Mission.

NEWSPAPERS AND TELEVISION CHANNELS

Depending on where you are in Australia there are up to five television stations:

♦ three commercial channels – 7, 9, 10 (in the capital cities)

- one ABC channel – 2
- one multicultural station – SBS on UHF channel 0/23.

There are numerous AM band radio stations including stations produced by the ABC – Australian Broadcasting Corporation. There are over 20 languages on multicultural stations and some city stations also specialise in services for disabled people. The FM band has an assortment of mainstream, rock, ABC and community radio stations.

There are two national newspapers:

- *The Financial Review*
- *The Australian.*

However each state also has its own publications:

Sydney
- *Sydney Morning Herald*
- *Telegraph Mirror*

Melbourne
- *Melbourne Age*
- *Herald Sun*

Adelaide
- *Advertiser*

Brisbane
- *Courier Mail*

Perth
- ◆ *Western Australian*

Hobart
- ◆ *Mercury*

Since Australia is such an ethnically diverse society,- newspapers and television and radio programmes are available in a number of community languages.

MEDICAL AND HEALTH SERVICES FOR VISITORS

Within Australia there is a high standard of medical, dental and hospital care that is on par with the best in the world and these services are readily available, but most overseas travellers should be aware that they are not covered by the free government Medicare system. Comprehensive travel and health insurance is therefore strongly recommended, as the bills can be high.

The telephone directory will list public hospitals, dentists, after hours medical and pharmaceutical services as well as Poisons Information Service. Please note that Australia does have several poisonous snakes and spiders, but there are not really any other dangerous animals except in the far north where you need to be aware of crocodiles. Danger zones for these reptiles are well signposted.

The Australian sunlight is amongst the strongest in the world, especially in the middle of summer. Always wear sunscreen lotion and a hat and avoid sunbathing in the middle of the day.

Pharmacies or chemists sell prescribed medication, general medication, cosmetics and toiletries. They are qualified specialists who are able to advise, dispense and sell the above mentioned medications. There are some late night chemists available within the inner cities, while in the small towns and suburbs they work on a roster system so at least one is open for a few hours over the weekend.

LANGUAGE

English is the official language of Australia. However, as the population make up is so ethnically diverse, you are sure to hear a large number of community languages spoken as well. In total there are about 140 different languages, and some of the communities such as Greek, Italian and Chinese have been established and settled for a long time. Other languages like Vietnamese, Russian and Portuguese are more recent arrivals and are now growing rapidly. Unfortunately it is extremely rare to hear one of the native Aboriginal languages being used.

Whatever your first language is you will need English to communicate within Australian society. Day-to-day activities like shopping, education and doing business require a knowledge of English. There are an abundance of English courses that are available to you. The Department of Immigration and Multicultural Affairs, tertiary institutes like TAFE – Tertiary And Further Education – and privately run English schools will all offer courses to cater for your requirements. Some courses are run during the day, but there will be courses you can find that are open after business hours.

OTHER USEFUL INFORMATION

Places of worship
There is a Catholic and an Anglican Church in every village, town and city within Australia. United churches are also common, but for many other religions you will only find mosques, temples and churches in major cities and some local communities.

Tipping
Tipping in Australia is not compulsory and is generally only expected in taxis and larger more expensive hotels and restaurants.

Opening times
+ Banks are generally open between 9.30am and 4pm.

+ Office hours throughout Australia are generally 9am to 5pm.

+ Shops open between 8 and 9am and close between 5 and 6pm. They open on Saturday morning and it is becoming increasingly popular to stay open into the afternoon. There is at least one late night shopping day in most major cities and it tends to be either Thursday or Friday.

+ Small grocery stores and petrol stations offer basic food and fuel and are open longer hours; some are becoming 24 hours a day, seven days a week.

+ Post offices are open from 9am to 5pm from Monday to Friday.

Telephone numbers
Australia has an excellent public telephone service with

phones available almost everywhere. Most phones accept cash but you can buy phone cards from kiosks, convenience stores, post offices and many other shops.

Emergency calls for fire, police and ambulance services can be made by dialling 000 anywhere in Australia – this is a 24-hour number.

Student and youth travel
In order to be eligible for discounts on travel and admission to attractions, you must be able to provide student identification. If you are from a foreign country you should carry an International Student Identity Card. As Australia has a widespread network of youth hostels and backpacker hostels young visitors are advised to join the International Youth Hostels Federation before leaving their home country.

Disabled visitors
Australia is very aware of the needs of disabled people. Advance notice is the best advice to give for anyone requiring any of the following services as they are available, you just need to book. You should be able to get help with:

♦ travel to and from the airport, railway or your accommodation
♦ cinemas
♦ restaurants
♦ special taxis
♦ rental cars.

Senior citizens
The general acceptance age for a senior citizen in

Australia is 60 or 65 years of age. Many attractions offer a discount and your passport should act as sufficient evidence. Unfortunately few discounts are available on the public transport system, as you need an Australian Pension Card and as a foreigner you are unable to apply for one.

Camping

All Australian campsites are inexpensive and accept tents, campervans and caravans. The amenities are normally clean and well kept. The only exception to this would be the National Parks where the campsite may simply be an area set aside for bush camping. Most campsites also have on-site vans available to rent, and this can work out to be a cheaper alternative to a hotel or motel. The main advantage of coastal sites is that they are normally found right on the edge of a beach. National Park offices are located in each state and offer advice, information and maps. The best place to look if you want to hire or buy campervans or holiday equipment is in the *Yellow Pages*, which can be found at Information Offices or at your hotel or motel.

What to wear

Overall the Australian lifestyle is very relaxed and dress codes tend to reflect this attitude as restaurants and nightclubs accept neat casual clothes. Business activities are still performed in a suit and tie except for in the very far north where the weather is so hot it is inappropriate – shorts and open neck shirts are the way to go.

Useful Contacts

We would suggest that the most up-to-date information regarding migration to Australia can be found at the Australian government website, www.immi.gov.au

Below are details of all DIMIA offices outside of Australia. These offices are able to process applications, give immigration information and issue visas to successful applicants:

COUNTRY	INTERNET/EMAIL
Argentina – Buenos Aires	www.argentina.embassy.gov.au
Austria – Vienna	www.austrian.embassy.at
Bangladesh – Dhaka	dima-dhaka@dfat.gov.au
Belgium – Brussels	www.austgov.fr
Brazil – Brasilia	dima-brasilia@dfat.gov.au
Brunei Darussalam – Bandar Seri Begawan	dima-brunei@dfat.gov.au
Burma (renamed Myanmar) – Rangoon	dima-rangoon@dfat.gov.au
Cambodia – Phnom Penh	dima-phnom.penh@dfat.gov.au
Canada – Ottawa	www.ahc-ottawa.org/visa
Chile – Santiago	dima-santiago@dfat.gov.au
Cyprus – Nicosia	dima-nicosia@dfat.gov.au
Egypt – Cairo	dima-cairo@dfat.gov.au
Federal Republic of Yugoslavia – Belgrade	dima-belgrade@dfat.gov.au
Fiji – Suva	dima-suva@dfat.gov.au
France – Paris	www.austgov.fr

Germany – Berlin	www.australian-embassy.de
Greece – Athens	dima-athens@dfat.gov.au
Hungary – Budapest	dima-budapest@dfat.gov.au
India – New Delhi	dima-new.delhi@dfat.gov.au
Indonesia – Jakarta	dima-bali@dfat.gov.au
Iran – Tehran	dima-tehran@dfat.gov.au
Ireland – Dublin	dima-dublin@dfat.gov.au
Israel – Tel Aviv	dima-tel.aviv@dfat.gov.au
Italy – Rome	dima-rome@dfat.gov.au
Japan – Tokyo	dima-tokyo@dfat.gov.au
Jordan – Amman	DIMIA-Amman@dfat.gov.au
Kenya – Nairobi	dima-nairobi@dfat.gov.au
Kiribati – Tarawa	dima-tarawa@dfat.gov.au
Korea – Seoul	dima-seoul@dfat.gov.au
Laos – Vientiane	dima-vientiane@dfat.gov.au
Lebanon – Beirut	dima-beirut@dfat.gov.au
Malaysia – Kuala Lumpur	dima-kuala.lumpar@dfat.gov.au
Malta – Malta	dima-malta@dfat.gov.au
Mauritius – Port Louis	dima-port.louis@dfat.gov.au
Mexico – Mexico City	dima-mexico.city@dfat.gov.au
Netherlands – The Hague	dima-the.hague@dfat.gov.au
New Caledonia – Noumea	dima-noumea@dfat.gov.au
New Zealand – Auckland	dima-auckland@dfat.gov.au
Nigeria – Lagos	dima-lagos@dfat.gov.au
Pakistan – Islamabad	dima-islamabad@dfat.gov.au
Papua New Guinea – Port Moresby	dima-port.moresby@dfat.gov.au
People's Republic of China	
– Beijing	dima-beijing@dfat.gov.au
– Hong Kong	dima-hongkong@dfat.gov.au
– Shanghai	dima-shanghai@dfat.gov.au
Philippines – Manila	dima-manila@dfat.gov.au
Poland – Warsaw	dima-warsaw@dfat.gov.au
Portugal –Lisbon	dima-lisbon@dfat.gov.au
Russia – Moscow	dima-moscow@dfat.gov.au
Samoa – Apia	dima-apia@dfat.gov.au
Singapore – Singapore	dima-singapore@dfat.gov.au
Solomon Islands – Honiara	dima-honiara@dfat.gov.au
South Africa – Pretoria	dima-pretoria@dfat.gov.au
Spain – Madrid	dima-madrid@dfat.gov.au

Sri Lanka – Colombo	dima-colombo@dfat.gov.au
Taiwan – Taipei	dima-taipei@dfat.gov.au
Thailand – Bangkok	dima-bangkok@dfat.gov.au
Timor (East) – Dili	dima-dila@dfat.gov.au
Tonga – Nuku'alofa	dima-nuku'alofa@dfat.gov.au
Turkey – Ankara	dima-ankara@dfat.gov.au
– Istanbul	dima-ankara@dfat.gov.au
United Arab Emirates – Dubai	dima-dubai@dfat.gov.au
United Kingdom – London	www.australia.org.uk
United States – Washington	www.austemb.org
Vanuatu – Port Villa	dima-port.villa@dfat.gov.au
Vietnam – Hanoi	dima-hanoi@dfat.gov.au
Zimbabwe – Harare	dima-harare@dfat.gov.au

GETTING HELP WITHIN AUSTRALIA

If you have travelled to Australia and need information once you have arrived then the DIMIA World Index has contact details for places within Australia.

Australia migration offices

Queensland
– Brisbane
– Cairns
– Southport
– Thursday Island

South Australia
–Adelaide

Western Australian
–Perth

Tasmania
–Hobart

New South Wales
–Parramatta
–Rockdale
–The Rocks
–On Shore Protection

Victoria
–Melbourne
–City Centre
–Dandedong
–Preston

Northern Territory
–Darwin

Australian Capital Territory
–ACT Regional Office
–Central Office

ENGLISH LANGUAGE TESTS

Should you be requested to undergo an English language test the following addresses will be useful:

Country	Contact details
Albania	elsona@icc.al.eu.org
Algeria	Fax: 32230067
Angola	Fax: 32333331
Argentina	Fax: 313117747
Australia	pullyng@janus.cqd.edu.au

There are also IELTS centres in the following locations. You will be able to locate these addresses on www.immi.-gov.au

Adelaide	Cairns	Newcastle	Townsville
Armidale	Darwin	Perth	Wagga Wagga
Brisbane	Hobart	Southport	Wollongong
Canberra	Melbourne	Sydney	

Austria	exams@bc-vienna.at
Bahrain	Fax: +241272
Bangladesh	DTO@The BritishCouncil.net
Belarus	Fax: +172364047
Belgium	Fax: +22270841
Bosnia	Fax: +00387 71 200890
Brazil	Fax: +41 224 1024
Brunei	Fax: +2453221
Bulgaria	Fax: +92 9434425
Burma	MayWin.Than@bc
Cambodia	palum.idpcam@bigpond.com.kh
Cameroon	Fax: +215691
Canada	Fax: +519 7483505
Chile	Fax: +56 2 2361199
China	bc.guangzhou@bc-gangzhou.sprint.com
Colombia	Fax: +12187754
Costa Rica	instbrit@sol.racsa.co.cr
Croatia	Fax: +385 1424888
Cyprus	bcexams.nicosia@britcoun.org.cy
Czech Republic	lucie.koranova@britcoun.cz or
	ivana.machajova@britcoun.cz
Denmark	Fax: +33321501
Eastern Adriatic	Dejana.Vukajlovic@britcoun.org.yu
Ecuador	dl@gye.satnet.net
Egypt	hala.eid@-alexandria.sprint.com
Eritrea	Fax: +11127230
Ethiopia	Fax: +1552544
Fiji	aidw@is.com.fj
Finland	Fax: +9629626
France	margaret.dalrymple@bc-paris.bcouncil.org

Germany	elfie.konrad@britcoun.de	
Ghana	Fax: +21663337	
Great Britain	Fax: 0207 815 1608	
Other offices in:		
Aberdeen	Cardiff	Manchester
Aberystwyth	Colchester	Norwich
Bath	Coventry	Nottingham
Belfast	Durham	Oxford
Birmingham	Edinburgh	Plymouth
Bournemouth	Exeter	Portsmouth
Brighton	Glasgow	Southampton
Bristol	Harrogate	Swansea
Cambridge	Leeds	York
Canterbury	Liverpool	
Greece	Fax: +31 282498 or +13 634769	
Hong Kong	www.education.com.hk/idp	
Hungary	Fax: +13425728	
India	Fax: +448523234 or +222852024	
Indonesia	fcargill@indosat.net.id	
Iran	mam@sinasoft.net	
Ireland	ALC@ucd.ie or Fax: +353 21 903 223	
Israel	Fax: +2283021 or +35221229	
Italy	Fax: +39 064814296 or +39 064814296	
Jamaica	Fax: +1876 9297090	
Japan	edaust@gol.com	
Jordan	Fax: +6656413	
Kazakhstan	Fax: +3272633339	
Kenya	Fax: +2339854	
Korea	Fax: +82514425435 or +8227738063	
Kuwait	Fax: +2520069	
Lao PDR	vtcollege@laonet.net	
Latvia	Fax: +7830031	
Lebanon	Fax: +1864534	
Lithuania	monika@bc-vilnius.ot.lt	
Madagascar	Fax: +226690	
Malaysia	info@johorbahru.idp.edu.au	

Mali	Fax: +2222214
Malta	admin@chamber-commerce.org.mt
Mauritius	Fax: +4549553
Mexico	marilu.groenwold@bc-mexico.bcouncil.org
Mongolia	Fax: +761358659
Morocco	britcoun.morocco.bcmor.org.ma
Mozambique	Fax: +1421577
Namibia	Fax: +61227530
Nepal	Fax: +1224076
Netherlands	Fax: +206264962
New Zealand	monasterioj@rimul.chchp.ac.nz
Other offices in:	
Auckland	
Dunedin	
Hamilton	
Palmerston North	
Wellington	
Nigeria	Fax: +422 501 58
Norway	Fax: +51534856
Oman	Fax: +212508 or +699163
Pakistan	aeo@khi.compol.com
Panama	Fax: +230730
Paraguay	Fax: +21203871
Peru	postmaster@bc-lima.org.pe
Phillipines	Fax: +63 2 815 9875
Poland	Fax: +26219955
Portugal	Fax: +315 2 208 3068
Qatar	Fax: +423315
Romania	Fax: +40 1210 0310
Russia	bc.moscow@bc-moscow.sprint.com
Saudi Arabia	Fax: +38268753 or +26726341
Senegal	Fax: +221 821 8136
Singapore	info@singapore.idp.edu.au
Slovakia	Fax: +7 533 47 05
Slovenia	info@britishcouncil.si
South Africa	Fax: +313057335 or +021 462 3960

Spain	Fax: +44762016 or +71172552
Sri Lanka	Fax: +1587079
Sudan	Fax: +11774935
Sweden	Fax: +8344192
Switzerland	Fax: +31 3011459
Syria	Fax: +963 11 332 1467
Taiwan	info@taipei.idp.edu.au
Thailand	austcent@loxinfo.co.th
Tunisia	Fax: +1353985
Turkey	Fax: +2122527474
Ukraine	Fax: +0442945507
United Arab Emirates	Fax: +2664340
Uruguay	Fax: +2921387
Venezuela	Fax: +58 2 952 9691
Vietnam	Fax: +84 8 846 5573
Yemen	Fax: +1244120
Zimbabwe	Fax: +4737877

Glossary

OCCUPATIONS LIST

Managers and administrators

Occupation	ASCO code	Assessing authority	Points for skill
Child Care Co-ordinator	1295-11	VETASSESS	50
Company Secretary	1212-11	VETASSESS	50
Construction Project Manager	1191-11	VETASSESS	50
Director of Nursing	1292-11	ANC	60
Education Manager (NEC)*	1293-79	VETASSESS	50
Engineering Manager	1221-11	IEA/AIM	60
Environment, Parks and Land Care Manager	1299-17	VETASSESS	50
Finance Manager	1211-11	CPAA/ACCA/NIA	60
General Manager	1112-11	AIM	60
Human Resources Manager	1213-11	AIM	60
Information Technology Manager	1224-11	ACS	60
Laboratory Manager	1299-13	VETASSESS	50
Medical Administrator	1292-13	VETASSESS	50
Policy and Planning Manager	1291-11	VETASSESS	50
Production Manager (Manufacturing)	1222-11	VETASSESS	60
Production Manager (Mining)	1222-13	VETASSESS	60
Project Builder	1191-13	VETASSESS	50
Regional Education Manager	1293-15	VETASSESS	50
Research and Development Manager	1299-11	VETASSESS	50
Sales and Marketing Manager	1231-11	AIM	60
Sports Administrator	1299-19	VETASSESS	50
Supply and Distribution Manager	1223-11	AIM	60
Welfare Centre Manager	1299-15	VETASSESS	50
Accountant	2211-11	CPAA/ICCA/NIA	60
Accountant – Corporate Treasurer	2213-11	CPAA/ICCA/NIA	60
Accountant – External Auditor	2212-11	CPAA/ICAA/NIA	60
Accountant – Internal Auditor	2212-13	VETASSESS	50
Actuary	2293-15	VETASSESS	50

*not elsewhere classified

Occupation	ASCO code	Assessing authority	Points for skill
Acupuncturist	2394-13	VETASSESS	50
Advertising Specialist	2221-17	VETASSESS	50
Agricultural Economist	2522-11	VETASSESS	50
Agricultural Engineer	2129-13	IEAust	60
Agricultural Engineering Technologist	2128-79	IEAust	60
Anatomist/Psychologist	2113-11	VETASSESS	50
Architect	2121-11	AACA	60
Architect – Landscape	2121-13	VETASSESS	50
Archivist	2299-15	VETASSESS	50
Audiologist	2399-11	VETASSESS	50
Biochemist	2113-17	VETASSESS	50
Botanist	2113-13	VETASSESS	50
Building Surveyor	NONE	VETASSESS	50
Business and Information Professionals (NEC)*	2299-79	VETASSESS	50
Cartographer	2123-11	VETASSESS	50
Chemist	2111-11	VETASSESS	50
Chiropractor	2387-11	SCORB	60
Community Worker	2512-13	VETASSESS	50
Conservator	2549-11	VETASSESS	50
Counsellors – Careers	2513-17	VETASSESS	50
Counsellors – Drugs and Alcohol	2513-13	VETASSESS	50
Counsellors – Family	2513-15	VETASSESS	50
Counsellors – Rehabilitation	2513-11	VETASSESS	50
Counsellors (NEC)*	2513-79	VETASSESS	50
Dental Specialist	2381-13	ADC	60
Dentist	2381-11	ADC	60
Designers and Illustrators – Fashion Designer	2533-11	VETASSESS	50
Designers and Illustrators – Graphic Designer	2533-13	VETASSESS	50
Designers and Illustrators – Illustrator	2533-19	VETASSESS	50
Designers and Illustrators – Industrial Designer	2533-15	VETASSESS	50
Designers and Illustrators – Interior Designer	2533-17	VETASSESS	50
Dietician	2393-11	DAA	60
Economist	2522-11	VETASSESS	50
Electorate Officer	2549-13	VETASSESS	50
Engineer – Aeronautical	2129-11	IEAust	60
Engineer – Agricultural	2129-13	IEAust	60
Engineer – Biomedical	2129-15	IEAust	60
Engineer – Building and Professionals (NEC)*	2129-79	IEAust	60

*not elsewhere classified

Occupation	ASCO code	Assessing authority	Points for skill
Engineer – Chemical	2129-17	IEAust	60
Engineer – Civil	2124-11	IEAust	60
Engineer – Civil Technologist	2128-11	IEAust	60
Engineer – Electrical	2125-11	IEAust	60
Engineer – Electrical or Electronics Technologist	2128-15	IEAust	60
Engineer – Electronics	2125-13	IEAust	60
Engineer – Engineering Technologist (NEC)*	2128-79	IEAust	60
Engineer – Industrial	2129-29	IEAust	60
Engineer – Materials	2127-15	IEAust	60
Engineer – Mechanical	2126-11	IEAust	60
Engineer – Mechanical Technologist	2128-13	IEAust	60
Engineer – Mining (excluding Petroleum)	2127-11	IEAust	60
Engineer – Naval Architect	2129-21	IEAust	60
Engineer – Petroleum	2127-13	IEAust	60
Engineer – Production or Plant Engineer	2126-13	IEAust	60
Environmental Health Officer	2543-13	VETASSESS	50
Extractive Metallurgist	2119-15	VETASSESS	50
Geologist	2112-11	VETASSESS	50
Geophysicist	2112-13	VETASSESS	50
Health Information Manager	2299-11	VETASSESS	50
Historian	2529-11	VETASSESS	50
Health Professionals (NEC)*	2399-79	VETASSESS	50
Industrial Relations Officer	2291-15	VETASSESS	50
Information Technology Officer – Applications and Analyst Programmer	2231-17	ACS	60
Information Technology Officer – Computer Systems Auditor	2231-21	ACS	60
Information Technology Officer – Computer Professionals (NEC)*	2231-79	ACS	60
Information Technology Officer – Software Designer	2231-15	ACS	60
Information Technology Officer – Systems Designer	2231-13	ACS	60
Information Technology – Systems Manager	2231-11	ACS	60
Information Technology Officer – Systems Programmer	2231-19	ACS	60
Intelligence Officer	2299-19	VETASSESS	50
Interpreter	2529-13	NAATI	60
Journalist – Copywriter	2534-19	VETASSESS	50

*not elsewhere classified

Occupation	ASCO code	Assessing authority	Points for skill
Journalist – Editor	2534-11	VETASSESS	50
Journalist – Print	2534-13	VETASSESS	50
Journalist – Radio	2534-17	VETASSESS	50
Journalist – Technical Writer	2534-21	VETASSESS	50
Journalist – Television	2534-15	VETASSESS	50
Journalist and Related Professionals (NEC)*	2534-79	VETASSESS	50
Land Economist	2295-13	VETASSESS	50
Legal Practitioner – Barrister	2521-11	SLAA	60
Legal Practitioner – Solicitor	2521-13	SLAA	60
Librarian	2292-11	VETASSESS	50
Life Scientist (NEC)*	2113-79	VETASSESS	50
Management Consultant	2294-11	VETASSESS	50
Marine Biologist	2113-19	VETASSESS	50
Market Research Analyst	2221-15	VETASSESS	50
Marketing Specialist	2221-13	VETASSESS	50
Master Fisher	2542-13	VETASSESS	40
Materials Scientist	2119-19	VETASSESS	50
Mathematician	2293-11	VETASSESS	50
Medical Practitioner – General Medical Practitioner Board	2311-11	State/Territory Medical	60
Medical Practitioner – Anaesthetist Board	2312-11	State/Territory Medical	60
Medical Practitioner – Dermatologist Board	2312-13	State/Territory Medical	60
Medical Practitioner – Emergency Medicine Specialist Board	2312-15	State/Territory Medical	60
Medial Practitioner – Obstetrician and Gynaecologist Board	2312-17	State/Territory Medical	60
Medical Practitioner – Opthamologist Board	2312-19	State/Territory Medical	60
Medical Practitioner – Paediatrician Board	2312-21	State/Terriory Medical	60
Medical Practitioner – Pathologist Board	2312-23	State/Territory Medical	60
Medical Practitioner – Specialist Physician Board	2312-25	State/Territory Medical	60
Medical Practitioner – Psychiatric Board	2312-27	State/Territory Medical	60
Medical Practitioner – Surgeon Board	2312-31	State/Territory Medical	60
Medical Practitioner – Special Medical Practitioners (NEC) *Board	2312-79	State/Territory Medical	60
Medical Scientist	2115-11	AIMS	60
Meteorologist	2119-13	VETASSESS	50

*not elsewhere classified

Occupation	ASCO code	Assessing authority	Points for skill
Museum or Gallery Curator	2549-21	VETASSESS	50
Natural/Physical Science Professionals (NEC)*	2119-79	VETASSESS	50
Naturopath	2394-11	VETASSESS	50
Nurse – Registered Developmental Disability	2326-11	ANC	60
Nurse – Registered Mental Health	2325-11	ANC	60
Nurse – Registered Midwife	2324-11	ANC	60
Nurse – Registered Nurse	2323-11	ANC	60
Occupational Health and Safety Officer	2543-11	VETASSESS	50
Occupational Therapist	2383-11	COTRB	60
Oenologist	2549-17	VETASSESS	50
Optometrist	2384-11	OCANZ	60
Organisation and Methods Analyst	2294-13	VETASSESS	50
Orthopist	2399-13	VETASSESS	50
Orthotist	2399-15	VETASSESS	50
Osteopath	2387-13	NOOSR	60
Patents Examiner	2549-15	VETASSESS	50
Personnel Consultant	2291-13	VETASSESS	50
Personnel Officer	2291-11	VETASSESS	50
Pharmacist – Hospital	2382-11	APEC	60
Pharmacist – Industrial	2382-13	VETASSESS	50
Pharmacist – Retail	2382-15	APEC	60
Physical Metallurgist	2119-17	VETASSESS	50
Physicist	2119-11	VETASSESS	50
Physiotherapist	2385-11	ACOPRA	60
Pilot – Aircraft	2541-11	CASA	60
Podiatrist	2388-11	APC	60
Policy Analyst	2299-17	VETASSESS	50
Psychologist – Clinical	2514-11	APS	60
Psychologist – Educational	2514-13	APS	60
Psychologist- Organisational	2514-15	APS	60
Psychologists (NEC)*	2514-79	APS	60
Public Relations Officer	2221-11	VETASSESS	50
Quality Assurance Manager	2294-15	VETASSESS	50
Quantity Surveyor	2122-11	AIQS	60
Radiographer – Medical Diagnostic	2391-11	AIR	60
Radiographer – Nuclear Medicine Technologist	2391-15	ANZSNM	60
Radiographer – Radiation Therapist	2391-13	AIR	60
Radiographer – Sonographer	2391-17	AIR	60
Records Manager	2299-13	VETASSESS	50
Recreation Officer	2549-19	VETASSESS	50

*not elsewhere classified

Occupation	ASCO code	Assessing authority	Points for skill
Sales Representative – Industrial Products	2222-11	VETASSESS	50
Sales Representative – Information and Communication Products	2222-13	VETASSESS	50
Sales Representative – Medical and Pharmaceutical Products	2222-15	VETASSESS	50
Sales Representative – Technical (NEC)*	2222-79	VETASSESS	50
Seafarer – Ship's Engineer	2542-15	AMSA	40
Seafarer – Ship's Master	2542-11	AMSA	40
Seafarer – Ship's Officer	2542-19	AMSA	40
Seafarer – Ship's Surveyor	2542-17	AMSA	40
Social Professionals (NEC)*	2529-79	VETASSESS	50
Social Worker	2511-11	AASW	60
Speech Pathologist	2386-11	SPA	60
Statistician	2293-13	VETASSESS	50
Surveyor	2123-13	ISA	60
Teacher – Art (Private)	2491-11	VETASSESS	50
Teacher – Dance (Private)	2491-15	VETASSESS	50
Teacher – Drama (Private)	2491-17	VETASSESS	50
Teacher – Education Officer	2493-11	VETASSESS	50
Teacher – Music (Private)	2491-13	VETASSESS	50
Teacher – Pre-Primary School	2411-11	NOOSR	60
Teacher – Primary School	2412-11	NOOSR	60
Teacher – Secondary School	2413-11	NOOSR	60
Teacher – Vocational Education (non trades)	2422-11	VETASSESS	50
Teacher – Vocational Education (trades)	2422-11	TRA	60
Training Officer	2291-17	VETASSESS	50
Translator	2529-15	NAATI	60
Urban and Regional Planner	2523-11	VETASSESS	50
Valuer	2295-11	VETASSESS	50
Veterinarian	2392-11	NOOSR	60
Welfare Worker	2512-11	AIWCW	60
Zoologist	2113-15	VETASSESS	50

Associate Professionals

Occupation	ASCO code	Assessing Authority	Points for skill
Aboriginal and Torres Straits Islander Health Worker	3493-11	VETASSESS	40
Ambulance Officer	3491-11	VETASSESS	40
Architectural Associate	3121-13	VETASSESS	40

*not elsewhere classified

Occupation	ASCO code	Assessing authority	Points for skill
Biomedical Engineering Associate	3129-11	IEAust	40
Branch Accountant (Financial Institution)	3211-11	VETASSESS	40
Building Associate Professional (NEC)*	3129-79	VETASSESS	40
Building Associate	312-11	VETASSESS	40
Building Inspector	3121-17	VETASSESS	40
Chef	3322-11	TRA	60
Chef – Head Chef	3322-01	TRA	60
Chemistry Technical Officer	3112-11	VETASSESS	40
Civil Engineering Associate	3122-11	IEAust	40
Civil Engineering Technician	3122-13	IEAust	40
Commodities Trader	3212-17	VETASSESS	40
Computing Support Technician	3294-11	TRA	40
Dental Hygienist	3492-13	VETASSESS	40
Dental Technician	3492-15	TRA	60
Dental Therapist	3492-11	VETASSESS	40
Disabilities Services Officer	3421-17	VETASSESS	40
Electrical Engineering Associate	3123-11	IEAust	40
Electrical Engineering Technician	3123-13	TRA	40
Electronic Engineering Associate	3124-11	IEAust	40
Electronic Engineering Technician	3124-13	TRA	40
Engineering Associate Professional (NEC)*	3129-79	IEAust	40
Family Support Worker	3421-19	VETASSESS	40
Financial Dealers and Brokers (NEC)*	3212-79	VETASSESS	40
Financial Institution Branch Manager	3211-13	VETASSESS	40
Financial Investment Adviser	3213-11	VETASSESS	40
Financial Market Dealer	3213-15	VETASSESS	40
Futures Trader	3212-13	VETASSESS	40
Hotel or Motel Manager (Degree Level)	3323-11	VETASSESS	50
Hotel or Motel Manager (Diploma Level)	3323-11	VETASSESS	40
Insurance Broker	3212-19	VETASSESS	40
Intensive Care Ambulance Paramedic	3491-13	VETASSESS	40
Interior Decorator	3999-11	VETASSESS	40
Library Technician	3997-11	VETASSESS	40
Massage Therapist	3494-11	VETASSESS	40
Mechanical Engineering Associate	3125-11	IEAust	40
Mechanical Engineering Technician	3125-13	TRA	40
Mediall Laboratory Technical Officer	3111-11	AIMS	40
Metallurgical and Materials Technican	3129-13	VETASSESS	40
Mine Deputy	3129-15	VETASSESS	40
Museum or Art Gallery Technician	3999-13	VBTASSESS	40
Office Manager	3291-11	VETASSESS	40

*not elsewhere classified

Occupation	ASCO code	Assessing authority	Points for skill
Parole or Probation Officer	3421-11	VETASSESS	40
Plumbing Engineering Associate	3121-21	VETASSESS	40
Plumbing Inspector	3121-19	VETASSESS	40
Primary Products Inspector	3991-11	VETASSESS	40
Project or Programme Administrator	3292-11	VETASSESS	40
Property Manager	3293-13	VETASSESS	40
Real Estate Agency Manager	3293-11	VETASSESS	40
Real Estate Salesperson	3293-15	VETASSESS	40
Residential Care Officer	3421-15	VETASSESS	40
Safety Inspector	3992-11	VETASSESS	40
Stockbroking Dealer	3212-11	VETASSESS	40
Surveying and Cartographic Associate	3121-15	VETASSESS	40
Youth Worker	3421-13	VETASSESS	40

Tradespersons and related workers

Occupation	ASCO code	Assessing authority	Points for skill
Aircraft Maintenace Engineer – (Avionics)	4114-15	TRA	60
Aircraft Maintenance Engineer – (Mechanical)	4114-11	TRA	60
Aircraft Maintenance Engineer – (Structure)	4114-13	TRA	60
Aircraft Maintenance Engineer – Supervisor	4114-01	TRA	60
Automotive Electrician	4212-11	TRA	60
Automotive Electricians Supervisor	4212-01	TRA	60
Bakers and Pastrycooks – Baker	4512-11	TRA	60
Bakers and Pastrycooks – Pastrycook	4512-13	TRA	60
Bakers and Pastrycooks – Supervisor	4512-01	TRA	60
Binder and Finisher	4913-11	TRA	60
Boat Builder and Repairer	4981-13	TRA	60
Bricklayer	4414-11	TRA	60
Bricklayer – Supervisor	4144-01	TRA	60
Broadcast Transmitter Operator	4992-17	TRA	60
Business Machine Mechanic	4315-13	TRA	60
Buttermaker or Cheesemaker	4519-13	TRA	60
Cabinetmaker	4922-11	TRA	60
Cabinetmaker – Supervisor	4922-01	TRA	60
Cable Jointer	4313-13	TRA	60
Canvas Goods Maker	4944-13	TRA	60
Carpenter	4411-13	TRA	60
Carpenter and Joiner	4411-11	TRA	60
Joiner	4411-15	TRA	60
Carpentry and Joinery Tradesperson – Supervisor	4411-01	TRA	60

Occupation	ASCO code	Assessing authority	Points for skill
Clothing – Apparel Cutter	4941-17	TRA	60
Clothing – Dressmaker	4941-15	TRA	60
Clothing – General Clothing Tradesperson	4941-11	TRA	60
Clothing – Patternmaker – Grader (Clothing)	4941-19	TRA	60
Clothing – Tailor	4941-13	TRA	60
Communications Lineperson	4316-13	TRA	60
Communications Tradesperson – Supervisor	4316-01	TRA	60
Confectioner	4519-15	TRA	60
Cook	4513-11	TRA	60
Diesel Fuel Injection Technicians	4999-79	TRA	60
Electrical Powerline Tradesperson	4313-11	TRA	60
Electrical Distribution Tradesperson	4313-01	TRA	60
Electrician – General	4311-11	TRA	60
Electrician – Lift Mechanic	4311-15	TRA	60
Electrician (Special Class)	4311-13	TRA	60
Electrician – Supervisor	4311-01	TRA	60
Electronic Equipment Tradesperson	4315-11	TRA	60
Electronic and Office Equipment Tradesperson	4315-01	TRA	60
Electronic Instrument Tradesperson (Special Class)	4314-13	TRA	60
Engraver	4115-21	TRA	60
Electroplater	4126-13	TRA	60
Fibrous Plasterer	4412-11	TRA	60
Fibrous Plasterer – Supervisor	4412-01	TRA	60
Flat Glass Tradesperson	4982-11	TRA	60
Floor Finisher	4423-11	TRA	60
Floor Finisher – Supervisor	4423-01	TRA	60
Forging Tradesperson – Blacksmith	4123-11	TRA	60
Forging Tradesperson – Farrier	4123-13	TRA	60
Forging Tradesperson – Supervisor	4123-01	TRA	60
Furniture Finisher	4929-13	TRA	60
Furniture Upholsterer	4942-11	TRA	60
Gardener – General Gardener	4623-11	TRA	60
Gardener – Head Gardener	4623-01	TRA	60
Gardener – Landscape Gardener	4623-13	TRA	60
Gardener – Tree Surgeon	4623-15	TRA	60
Gem Cutter and Polisher	4983-13	TRA	60
General Communications Tradesperson	4316-11	TRA	60
General Electronic Instrument Tradesperson	4314-11	TRA	60

Occupation	ASCO code	Assessing authority	Points for skill
General Fabrication Engineering Tradesperson	4121-11	TRA	60
General Fabrication Engineering Tradesperson – Supervisor	4121-01	TRA	60
General Mechanical Engineering Tradesperson	4111-11	TRA	60
General Mechanical Engineering Tradesperson – Supervisor	4111-01	TRA	60
Glass Blower	4982-13	TRA	60
Graphic Pre-Press Tradesperson	4911-11	TRA	60
Greenkeeper	4622-11	TRA	60
Hairdresser	4931-11	TRA	60
Hairdresser – Supervisor	4931-01	TRA	60
Jeweller	4938-11	TRA	60
Leather Goods Maker	4944-11	TRA	60
Meat Tradesperson – Butcher	4511-11	TRA	60
Meat Tradesperson – Smallgoods Maker	4511-13	TRA	60
Meat Tradesperson – Supervisor	4511-01	TRA	60
Medical Grade Shoemaker	4943-13	TRA	60
Metal Casting Tradesperson	4125-11	TRA	60
Metal Casting Tradesperson – Supervisor	4125-01	TRA	60
Metal Fitters and Machinists – Fitter	4112-11	TRA	60
Metal Fitters and Machinists – Metal Machinist (First class)	4112-13	TRA	60
Metal Fitters and Machinists Textile, Clothing or Footwear	4112-15	TRA	60
Metal Fitters and Machinists – Supervisor	4112-01	TRA	60
Metal Finishing Tradesperson – Metal Polisher	4126-11	TRA	60
Metal Finishing Tradesperson – Supervisor	4126-01	TRA	60
Motor Mechanic	4211-11	TRA	60
Motor Mechanic – Supervisor	4211-01	TRA	60
Nurseryperson	4621-11	TRA	60
Optical Mechanic	4999-11	TRA	60
Painter and Decorator	4421-11	TRA	60
Painter and Decorator – Supervisor	4421-01	TRA	60
Panel Beater	4213-11	TRA	60
Panel Beater – Supervisor	4213-01	TRA	60
Piano Tuner	4999-17	TRA	60
Picture Framer	4929-11	TRA	60

Occupation	ASCO code	Assessing authority	Points for skill
Plumber – Drainer	4431-15	TRA	60
Plumber – Gasfitter	4431-13	TRA	60
Plumber – General Plumber	4431-11	TRA	60
Plumber – Mechanical Services and Airconditioning Plumber	4431-19	TRA	60
Plumber – Roof Plumber	4431-17	TRA	60
Plumber – Supervisor	4431-01	TRA	60
Precision Metal Tradesperson – Engraver	4115-21	TRA	60
Precision Metal Tradesperson – Gunsmith	4115- 19	TRA	60
Precision Metal Tradesperson – Locksmith	4115-15	TRA	60
Precision Metal Tradesperson – Precision Instrument Maker and Repairer	4115-11	TRA	60
Precision Metal Tradesperson – Saw Maker and Repairer	4115-17	TRA	60
Precision Metal Tradesperson – Watch and Clock Maker and Repairer	4115-13	TRA	60
Precision Metal Tradesperson – Supervisor	4115-01	TRA	60
Printing Machinist	4912-11	TRA	60
Refrigeration and Airconditioning Mechanic	4312-11	TRA	60
Refrigeration and Airconditioning Mechanic – Supervisor	4312-01	TRA	60
Roof Slater and Tiler	4413-11	TRA	60
Roof Slater and Tiler – Supervisor	4413-01	TRA	60
Sail Maker	4944-15	TRA	60
Screen Printer	4914-11	TRA	60
Sheetmetal Worker	4124-11	TRA	60
Sheetmetal Tradesperson – Supervisor	4124-01	TRA	60
Shipwright	4981-11	TRA	60
Shoemaker	4943-11	TRA	60
Signwriter	4422-11	TRA	60
Signwriter – Supervisor	4422-01	TRA	60
Small Offset Printer	4912-13	TRA	60
Solid Plasterer	4415-11	TRA	60
Solid Plasterer – Supervisor	4415-01	TRA	60
Stonemason	4416-13	TRA	60
Toolmaker	4113-11	TRA	60
Toolmaker – Supervisor	4113-01	TRA	60

Occupation	ASCO code	Assessing authority	Points for skill
Tradesperson and Related Workers (NEC)	4999-79	TRA	60
Upholsterer and Bedding Tradesperson (NEC)	4942-79	TRA	60
Vehicle Body Maker	4215-11	TRA	60
Vehicle Body Maker – Supervisor	4215-01	TRA	60
Vehicle Painter	4214-11	TRA	60
Vehicle Painter – Supervisor	4214-01	TRA	60
Vehicle Trimmer	4216-11	TRA	60
Vehicle Trimmer – Supervisor	4216-01	TRA	60
Wall and Floor Tiler	4416-11	TRA	60
Wall and Floor Tiler and Stonemason	4416-01	TRA	60
Structural Steel and Welding Tradesperson – Metal Fabricator (Boilermaker)	4122-11	TRA	60
Structural Steel and Welding Tradesperson – Pressure Welder	4122-13	TRA	60
Structural Steel and Welding Tradesperson – Welder (First Class)	4122-15	TRA	60
Structural Steel and Welding Tradesperson – Welder (Supervisor)	4122-01	TRA	60
Wood Tradesperson (NEC)*	4929-79	TRA	60
Wood Turner	4921-13	TRA	60

*not elsewhere classified

Contact details of assessing authorities

AACA – Architects Accreditation Council of Australia Incorporated

Email: registrar@aaca.org.au

Website: www.aaca.org.au

AASW – Australian Association of Social Workers

Email: aaswosea@aasw.asn.au

Website: www.aasw.asn.au

ACOPRA – Australian Council of Physiotherapy Regulatory Authority

Email: acopra@acopra.com.au

Website: www.acopra.com.au

ACS – Australian Computer Society
Email: info@acs.org.au
Website: www.acs.org.au

ADC – Australian Dental Council
Email: info@dentalcouncil.net.au
Website: www.dentalcouncil.net.au

AIM – Australian Institute of Management
Email: barbarak@aim.com.au
Website: www.aim.com.au

AIMS – Australian Institute of Medical Scientists
Email: aimsnat@medeserv.com.au
Website: www.aims.org.au

AIQS – Australian Institute of Quantity Surveyors
Email: AIQS@compuserve.com
Website: www.aiqs.com.au

AIR – Australian Institute of Radiography
Email: air@A-I-R.com.au
Website: www.A-I-R.com.au

AIWCW – Australian Institute of Welfare and Community Workers
Email: aiwcw@ozemail.com.au
Website: www.aiwcw.org.au

AMSA – Australian Maritime Safety Authority
Email: maritime.qualifications@amsa.gov.au
Website: www.amsa.gov.au

ANC – Australian Nursing Council Incorporated
Email: anci@anc.org.au
Website: www.anc.org.au

ANZSNM – Australian and New Zealand Society of Nuclear Medicine Incorporated
Email: anzsnm@21century.com.au
Website: www.anzsnm.org.au

APodC – Australasian Podiatry Council
Email: apodc@ozemail.com.au
Website: www.apodc.com.au

APEC – Australian Pharmacy Examining Council Incorporated
Email: registrar@apec.asn.au
Website: www.apec.asn.au

APS – Australian Psycholgical Society
Email: membership@psychsociety.com.au
Website: www.aps.psychosociety.com.au

AVBC – Australian Veterinary Boards Council Incorporated
Email: avbc@ozemail.com.au
Website: www.avbc.asn.au

CASA – Civil Aviation Safety Authority
Email: fcl.licensing@casa.gov.au
Website: www.casa.gov.au

COTRB – Council of Occupational Therapists Registration Board Incorporated

Email: cotrb@seret.com.au
Website: www.cotrb.com

CPAA – Certified Practising Accountants of Australia
Email: osassess@cpaaustralia.com.au
Website: www.cpaaustralia.com.au

DAA – Dieticians Association of Australian
Email: national office@daa.asn.au
Website: www.daa.asn.au

ICAA – Institute of Chartered Accountants of Australia
Email: assess@icaa.org.au
Website: www.icaa.org.au

IEAust – Institute of Engineers Australia
Email: osqa@ieaust.org.au
Website: www.ieaust.org.au

ISA – Institute of Surveyors, Australia
Email: isa@isaust.org.au
Website: www.isaust.org.au

NAATI – National Accreditation Authority for Translators and Interpreters
Website: www.naati.com.au

NIA – National Institute of Accountants
Email: natoffice@nia.org.au
Website: www.nia.org.au

NOOSR – National Office of Overseas Skills Recognition
Email: noosr@dest.gov.au
Website: www.dest.gov.au/noosr

OCANZ – Optometry Council of Australia and New Zealand
Email: ocanz@ozemail.com.au
Website: www.ocanz.org

SCORB – State Chiropractors/Osteopaths Registration Board
Refer to relevant State/Territory

SLAA – State Legal Admission Authority
Refer to relevant State/Territory

SPAA – Speech Pathology Association of Australia
Email: spaathau@vicnet.net.au
Website: www.speechpathologyaustralia.org.au

TRA – Trades Recognition Australia
Website: www.workplace.gov.au/tra

VETASSESS – Vocational Education and Training Assessment Services
Email: vetassess@vetassess.com.au
www.vetassess.com.au

Useful contact addresses

Queensland

Queensland Government	www.qld.gov.au
Department of State Development	www.statedevelopment.qld.gov.au
Queensland Industry Profiles	www.statedevelopment.qld.gov.au/invest/profiles/
Queensland Treasury	www.treasury.qld.gov.au
Statistics – Queensland	www.statistics.qld.gov.au
Department of Education	http://education.qld.gov.au
Department of Primary Industry	www.dpi.qld.gov.au

Information Industries Board   www.iib.qld.gov.au
Food Manufacture   www.food.qld.gov.au
Tourism   www.tq.com.au/research/websites.htm
Queensland Chamber of Commerce and Industry   www.qcci.com.au
Real Estate   www.homesonline.com.au
Industrial Relations   www.dtir.qld.gov.au
Wages and Allowances information
     www.dtir.qld.gov.au/ir/wagesh/wagesh.htm

Queensland regional information

(This list is not exhaustive)
Brisbane City   www.brisbane.qld.gov.au
Brisbane City Life   www.maxlink.com.au/bcl/
Gold Coast   www.goldcoast.qld.gov.au
Mackay   www.mackay.qld.gov.au
Maryborough   www.maryborough.qld.gov.au
Noosa (Sunshine Coast)   www.noosa.qld.gov.au
Rockhampton   www.rockhampton.qld.gov.au
Toowoomba   www.toowoomba.qld.gov.au
Townsville   www.townsville.qld.gov
Warwick   www.warwick.qld.gov

Australia

Australian Government   www.fed.gov.au
Business Entry Point   www.business.gov.au
How to register a company, etc (ASIC)
     www.asic.gov.au/info4companies/index.htm
Australia Bureau of Statistics   www.abs.gov.au
Australian Tax Office   www.ato.gov.au
Tax Reform (GST)   www.taxreform.ato.gov.au
Medicare   www.hic.gov.au
Australian Industry (incl industry profiles)   www.ausindustry.gov.au
Australian Trade Commission   www.austrade.gov.au
Australian Customs Services   www.customs.gov.au
Australian Info Industrial Association   www.aiia.com.au
Australian Institute of Engineers   www.ieaust.org.au
CSIRO (incl industrial information sheets)   www.csiro.us
Dept of Industry Science and Resources   www.disr.gov.au

Invest Australia   www.investaustralia.gov.au
Intellectual Property   www.ipaustralia.gov.au
ABC – news and weather   www.abc.net.au/news/weather/default.htm
The Australian – news and weather   www.news.com.au
Australian White Pages   www.whitepages.com.au
Australian Yellow Pages   www.yellowpages.com.au

Immigration

Department of Immigration   www.immi.gov.au
Migration Institute of Australia   www.mia.aust.com

Index